Fishing in British Columbia, with a chapter on tuna fishing at Santa Catalina

Thomas Wilson Lambert

Nabu Public Domain Reprints:

You are holding a reproduction of an original work published before 1923 that is in the public domain in the United States of America, and possibly other countries. You may freely copy and distribute this work as no entity (individual or corporate) has a copyright on the body of the work. This book may contain prior copyright references, and library stamps (as most of these works were scanned from library copies). These have been scanned and retained as part of the historical artifact.

This book may have occasional imperfections such as missing or blurred pages, poor pictures, errant marks, etc. that were either part of the original artifact, or were introduced by the scanning process. We believe this work is culturally important, and despite the imperfections, have elected to bring it back into print as part of our continuing commitment to the preservation of printed works worldwide. We appreciate your understanding of the imperfections in the preservation process, and hope you enjoy this valuable book.

FISHING
IN
BRITISH COLUMBIA.

FISHING
IN
BRITISH COLUMBIA

WITH A CHAPTER ON TUNA FISHING
AT SANTA CATALINA.

BY

T. W. LAMBERT,

M A , M B , B C (Cantab.), M.R C S., L.R C P. (London)

*Late Surgeon to the Western Division, Canadian
Pacific Railway Company.*

LONDON:
HORACE COX,
"FIELD" OFFICE, WINDSOR HOUSE, BREAM'S
BUILDINGS, E.C.
—
1907

LONDON
PRINTED BY HORACE COX, "FIELD" OFFICE, WINDSOR HOUSE,
BREAM'S BUILDINGS, E.C.

PREFACE.

THE Author hopes that this book may prove of some interest to anglers by giving a short account of the fishing which is to be obtained in a part of the world hitherto little exploited, and well worthy of better acquaintance.

British Columbia only became fairly easy of access after the completion of the Canadian Pacific Railway in 1887, which placed it within two weeks' journey from London. Before that time it was cut off by the immense prairies of the north-west of Canada, and could only be reached by a long journey round Cape Horn or over the Isthmus of Panama. Since the date given, however, a new era has dawned for the country, and all the southern part of it has been opened up by railways. Thus its waters have been rendered easy of access to any fisherman willing to try them. The position of the country on the map resembles that of Norway and Sweden in Europe, and the general resemblance is borne out by the features of both countries. Each possesses a deeply indented coast line and a wealth of pine forests, lakes, and rivers. But the climate of British Columbia is much milder; the valleys are richer in soil, the mountains in precious metals, and the waters are inhabited by different species of fish. And whereas the Scandinavian peninsula has some ten millions of people, British Columbia supports as yet but one hundred thousand of population, including Indians

It is without doubt a country of great possibilities. The summer climate of the southern central plateau is very bracing and dry, resembling that of the southern Californian winter; while the winter climate of the coast is like Devonshire. Game, both large and small, is still plentiful in the south, while the northern part is one of the best big game districts of the world.

British Columbia is the home of the rainbow trout, which flourishes in all its rivers and lakes to the furthest north, and spreads southwards into the neighbouring Pacific states, where it has, however, to compete with another species, the cut-throat trout. The eastern limit of the rainbow is the Rocky Mountain range.

The chief purpose of this book is to give some idea of the habits and peculiarities of the rainbow, and the sport which it affords in its native haunts. The author spent some twelve years in the interior of the country, and has fished a great many of its numberless lakes and streams, so he may claim to write from practical experience. But he writes also with the hope that perhaps someone more competent may in the future publish a complete history of this most interesting fish, and solve some of the problems which are here but alluded to. For there is ample scope in these almost virgin waters for both the naturalist and the fisherman, to whom these notes may perhaps serve as the blazes on a mountain trail, and as some slight record of the sport that was to be obtained in the earlier days of British Columbia.

Though the inland waters swarm with Pacific salmon at certain seasons, the fish are useless for purposes of sport. They take no bait of any kind when they have once started to migrate up the rivers. In the salt water, however, and while waiting at the mouths of rivers, they take a spoon-bait freely, and the smaller kinds will in the same conditions often rise readily to the fly. But it may be stated, as a general rule, no salmon are ever taken on bait or fly as they travel, and when they reach the upper waters.

The Dominion Government has recently tried

the experiment of hatching and turning out 250,000 of the small fry of the Atlantic salmon from one of their hatcheries; and, should success attend the effort, a great attraction would be added to the inland streams; but a period of some few years must naturally elapse before any opinion can be given as to the success or failure of this attempt.

British Columbia is reached as soon as the traveller crosses the summit of the Rocky Mountains, just beyond Banff, on the main line of the Canadian Pacific Railway. The summit, which is known as the Great Divide, separates the Pacific Slope from Eastern Canada. The crossing once made, a country is reached in which there is a great change in climate, fauna, and flora; and in the rivers, instead of the so-called speckled trout, the muskallunge, black bass, and Atlantic salmon, are found the rainbow, silver, and steel-head trout, with the five species of the Pacific salmon. This last fish is not a salmon at all, but only bears the title by courtesy, because no other Anglo-Saxon name has been given to it. The early settlers mistook it for a salmon, and called it a salmon because it so closely resembled one in appearance and habits, just as the ruffed grouse was, and is, called a partridge in Eastern Canada. But it has no true English name. Scientifically, the five species of Pacific "salmon" belong to the genus *Oncorhynchus*, and each is mostly called by the Indian name which distinguished it when the white man first arrived, such as *quinnat* or *cohoe*. The physical relationship of the Pacific *Oncorhynchus* to the Atlantic *Salmo salar* is not unlike the physical relationship of the grayling or char to the trout.

The rainbow is found before the Divide is reached, in some of the streams flowing eastward from the Rockies, but it does not follow them much below the foothills; and it abounds in the rivers and lakes among the mountains themselves. But it is not until the central plateau of British Columbia is reached, a country of rolling hills, valleys, and open range abounding in lakes and small streams, that the best fishing grounds are encountered, the true home and headquarters of the rainbow trout.

The streams and lakes in the mountains are too turbulent, and fed by too much glacier and snow-water, to make the best fishing grounds. The guide-books of the railway speak highly of the fishing through the mountains, but there is better to be obtained lower down, and my advice to the traveller is to make no stop for fishing purposes until Sicamous is reached, at the head of Shuswap Lake where the Eagle River enters it. The Thompson River flows out of the lake at the other end, and the Shuswap Lake and Thompson River constitute the best fishing district of British Columbia, and will be the chief subject of the following pages.

It should be premised, however, that there is plenty of what may be styled "virgin water" in British Columbia besides the streams and lakes described in these pages. In a few years the Grand Trunk Pacific Railway will render accessible a network of rivers and lakes some four hundred miles to the north of the present line, and the addition to the angler's opportunities by this will, of course, be very great.

The cost of the fourteen-day journey from London to British Columbia will be at most £50 each way; it can be done for much less. There is no charge for the fishing, and ordinary living expenses are not high. One can stop at the hotels along the Thompson for 2 dollars a day, in Kamloops for 3 dollars a day, in the Canadian Pacific Railway hotels at 4 dollars to 6 dollars. There are no extra charges, except at the bar, which in British Columbia it is considered the duty of everyone to support liberally. A stranger will find that a few dollars spent judiciously and with tact in this way will usually be productive of quite astonishing results. In the West a drink puts everyone on equal terms, and at once establishes a feeling of *camaraderie*. It might be said to correspond somewhat to the old custom of offering the snuffbox.

The natives understand it as a sign that the stranger wishes to be on good terms, that he does not consider himself superior in any sense, that there is no side about him, that he is willing to drink with them as an equal. He will certainly receive a like invitation, and he must on no account refuse; to do so is an unpardonable violation of Western etiquette, even if everyone present insists on taking the part of host in turn. There is, however, no cause for alarm on the score of temperance, for it is quite *de rigueur* to ask for a cigar or to take a mere apology for a drink. If the stranger thus satisfies Western ideas of what is right and proper he will usually find that the individuals who had apparently hitherto regarded him somewhat in the manner that a strange dog seems to be looked at by his fellows in a new street will quite suddenly be most interested in his pursuit and most willing to help him in every possible way with advice as to someone who can tell him all about the river or lake and the best way to get there. Perhaps even the result may be an offer of a horse or hospitality for a night or two from some ranchman who may live near the place he wishes to get to. The people of British Columbia are, as a rule, most generous and open-hearted when they are approached in the right way. All men are equal in the West; there must be no question of standing on one's dignity.

As regards outfit in general (fishing tackle is dealt with later), it is the greatest mistake to take a lot of useless luggage. Any rough fishing suit will do, and a strong pair of boots. Waders are not needed, except in the coast rivers. Everything can be got in the country itself The Hudson Bay stores or the general store which is found in every little town will provide everything that is wanted. My advice is to procure the outfit in the country itself, because they know best what is needed for the local wants.

CONTENTS.

CHAPTER I.

PAGE

The Rainbow Trout—Names—Distribution—Appearance—Size in British Columbia—Its Food—Fly-fishing for—Sporting Qualities—Possibility of New Species being Discovered   1

CHAPTER II.

Season for Trout Fishing—Principal Districts—Tackle Necessary—"No Drawing-room Work"—Advantage of Plenty of Time—Poor Fishing in the Rockies—The Thompson River—The South Thompson—Its Course and Character—Clear, Swift Water—Difficulty of Landing Big Fish—A Lost Thirty-pounder—The Successful Cherokee Fisherman—Fine, Calm Days Best for Fishing—Mosquitoes not Troublesome   ...   9

CHAPTER III.

The Kamloops District—Kamloops as Headquarters—May Floods and Fishing in Shuswap Lake—Silver-bodied Flies—Streams Running into the Lake—The Eagle River—Advantages of a Steam Launch—A Big Catch—Possibilities of the Prawn—A July Spectacle—Fishing at Tranquille—Kamloops Lake—Savona's Ferry—Great Sport in June—Dolly Varden Trout—A Fifteen-Pounder—Falling-off of Sport when Salmon are Running—The "Salmon Fly"—Size of Catches on the Thompson—August a Bad Month   20

CHAPTER IV.

What is the "Silver Trout"?—Evidence in Favour of a New Species—Difference in Appearance from the Rainbow—A Jumper—Native of Kamloops and Shuswap Lakes—A Bag of Twenty-four—The Dolly Varden—Origin of the Name—Not a Free Riser—Grayling—Chub and Squaw Fish—Great Lake Trout—The Silver Fish at Spence's Bridge—Salmon or Steel-head?—Cut-throat Trout—Possible Fishing Tour in British Columbia ... 34

CHAPTER V.

Other Lakes—Long Lake—Its Silvery Trout—Fish Lake—Extraordinary Fishing—Fifteen Hundred Trout in Three Days—A Miniature Gaff—Uses of a Collapsible Boat—Catching Fish Through the Ice—Mammit Lake—Nicola Lake—Beautifully Marked Trout in Nicola River—"The Little Red Fish" 46

CHAPTER VI

The Kootenay District—Sawdust and Dynamite—Fine Sport in Vancouver—Harrison River and Lake—Big Fish in the Coquehalla—The Steel-head in the Fraser—Need for Better River Protection ... 65

CHAPTER VII.

The Salmons of the Pacific—Legends Concerning Them—The Five Species—Systems of Migration—Powers of Endurance—Absence of Kelts—Do They Take a Fly?—Terrible Mortality—"A Vivid Red Ribbon"—Points of Difference Between the Quinnat and *Salmo salar*—Work of the Canneries—Artificial Propagation 72

Contents. XV

CHAPTER VIII.

PAGE

The Diplomat and the Salmon—The Struggle for Existence—Salmon and Steel-head Liable to be Confused—Sport in Tidal Waters—The Campbell River—The Pioneers—A River of Fifty-Pounders—Smaller Salmon on the Fly—Method of Fishing—Tackle—Typical Good Bags—The Steel-head—Cost of Fishing—Dangers of Over-Fishing for Canneries—A Good Trolling Time.. ... 91

CHAPTER IX.

Recapitulation of Salmon and Trout Problems—Importance of Preserving British Columbian Fisheries—Possibility of Introducing Atlantic Salmon—Question of Altering Present Close Season for Trout—Past and Present Neglect of Trout Fisheries—Need for Governmental Action—Difficulties in the Way of it—Conclusion ... 107

CHAPTER X.

Tuna Fishing at Avalon, Santa Catalina Island 118

FISHING IN BRITISH COLUMBIA.

CHAPTER I.

The Rainbow Trout—Names—Distribution—Appearance—Size in British Columbia—Its Food—Fly-fishing for—Sporting Qualities—Possibility of New Species being Discovered.

THE Rainbow trout (*Salmo irideus*) is a true trout of the same genus as, and closely allied to, the common trout (*S. fario*) of the British Isles, where it is also now acclimatised. It holds the same position in every stream, lake, and river of the northern part of the Pacific Coast of North America as the brown trout does in the United Kingdom. Unless the water, for some local reason, is unsuitable, it is met with everywhere, until further south it overlaps with the cut-throat trout, which ultimately seems to take its place.

In the small mountain streams it is very plentiful, and is generally called the brook, mountain, or speckled trout, and when of larger size is known locally as the "red side"—a name which often very aptly describes it. The name "rainbow" is not much heard or used locally.

In the different lakes and rivers the fish varies a good deal in size, numbers, colour, and appearance—so much so that when these waters are better known the naturalist may be inclined to name and describe several varieties of rainbows, perhaps even may discover new species.

This fish is confined to the west side of the Rocky Mountains, save in the head waters of the streams which take their source from these mountains and then flow east. Often two streams flow from a lake, one east and one west, and the rainbow is found in both; a good instance of this is found in the Kicking Horse and the Bow rivers. The latter flows east from the divide, and the rainbow follows it for some distance into the prairie, but as this river ceases to be a mountain stream and becomes sluggish and discoloured traces of the fish cease. But in the clear streams of Eastern Canada, near the great lakes, its place is taken by the spotted trout (*Salvelinus fontinalis*), a beautiful and game fish, member of the char family, unknown west of the Rockies.

In appearance the rainbow is well worthy of its name, and may justly claim to be the equal in beauty, if not the superior, of any of the Salmonidæ. It is clean-cut in shape, perhaps rather lither than the brown trout, and when large it is not so deep. The colour on the back is an olive green, with the usual characteristic black spots, and at the side a few red ones; laterally the green shades off into silver and sometimes gold, while along its side from gill to tail flashes the beautiful rainbow stripe, varying from pale sunset pink to the most vivid scarlet or crimson; often the effect is as if a paint-brush dipped in red paint had been drawn along the fish's side; the belly is silvery white; the anal, ventral, and pectoral fins being coloured in proportion to the colouring of the individual fish. The general appearance is very striking, and in a fine specimen is certainly one of great beauty. When fresh from the water and in brilliant sunshine the fish rivals the object after which it is called; the living rainbow on its side shows a play of delicate colour which it would be hard to surpass or to equal, even in the heavens.

From the fly-fisherman's point of view the fish may be said to run up to 4lb. in weight; by which statement it is meant that the fly is readily taken in both stream and lake by fish up to this size. Mr. F. J. Fulton, of Kamloops, states that he has never landed a 5lb fish on the fly, and he is an authority on the Thompson River. Personally, I have never seen a rainbow over 4lb. which I knew to have been caught with the fly; but I have seen a model of a fish of 12lb. caught with the fly in 1891 in Kamloops Lake by Captain Drummond. There is, of course, not the slightest doubt that the fish grows to a much larger size. Mr. Walter Langley caught a rainbow of 22½lb. on a small spoon in Marble Canyon Lake about May, 1900, and the photograph of this fish was published in the *Field*. I have also seen very big specimens which had been speared by Indians in the Thompson and sold as "salmon"; two of them I weighed myself and found to be 15lb. and 12lb. respectively. While, therefore, there is some evidence to show that these large fish may be caught with spoon and minnow, it may be stated as a broad fact that the rainbow is not often caught with the fly over the weight of 4lb., and that up to this size he takes it freely.

The fly is taken best during the months of June and July, when there is a rise of the stone fly in the rivers, and flies of all kinds are plentiful in the lakes. At this time, indeed, natural fly seems to be the main article of the fish's food. But the small fry of the salmon and of its own species are also devoured in great numbers, and in late summer there are grasshoppers as well; these are very plentiful, and are eagerly snapped up as they fall into the water. No doubt a further great source of food supply is the spawn of the salmon, which must be very plentiful on the spawning beds. It forms the usual lure of the Indian fishermen.

The feeding-grounds of the rainbow are the eddies and the back-washes in the swift-running rivers, into which flies, grasshoppers, and other food are carried by the current. A very favourite haunt is at the mouth of creeks and streams running into a lake, or where a large river runs into or out of a large lake. Food is naturally plentiful at such places, and at certain times the fish gather there in great numbers, splashing about and chasing the small fry. They will then take a silver-bodied fly most greedily.

In many of the smaller mountain lakes where fly seems to be at certain seasons the rainbow's sole food, no other lure will attract it, but with the fly great numbers may be caught. The flyfisher also scores among fish gathered at the mouths of creeks swollen by summer floods. The minnow, also, both natural and artificial, is useful in these conditions, and it will account for much larger fish, up to 10lb. and even over; these monsters have probably forsaken a fly diet and taken to small fry. But there is no doubt that the rainbow is, quite as much as our own trout, a fly-feeder, and that it takes the artificial as readily and, owing to want of education, and, perhaps, also to natural boldness, with even greater freedom and less regard to the nature of the lure or the skill of the fisherman who throws it.

So far as strength and gameness go the rainbow is fully the equal of the brown trout, and, in my opinion, its superior, though, as its play is often aided by the very strong water it frequents, its strength may sometimes appear greater than it would in our smaller streams. For this reason fishing for rainbows in British Columbia has always seemed to me to resemble sea-trout fishing more than the fishing for brown trout; perhaps less skill is necessary, but there is a stronger fight

The rivers and lakes of British Columbia are at present an angler's paradise, and will probably long continue to be so. And it promises the additional interest that the fisherman is not treading a beaten and well-known path. There is pioneer work for him to do. There are many problems for him to solve and discoveries for him to make. In the numberless lakes and rivers stretching far up through northern British

Columbia to the Arctic, it is not unlikely that several new species of the Salmonidæ await description.

The big-game hunter has shown what secrets may lie hid in so wide a land, for since these northern regions have been explored for big game and gold (from the date of the Klondike rush in 1898) no fewer than four new species of the sheep family have been discovered; a pure white mountain sheep, for instance, has been found to exist in great numbers. "Heads" of this sheep are now quite common, but it is a most curious proof of the general ignorance of the country ten years ago that such a remarkable animal was then entirely unknown. Had any explorer in those days reported seeing such an animal without bringing any tangible proof to support his story, he would have been universally regarded as a most unique liar, in a part of the world where such people are far from uncommon. The enormous moose heads recently brought down from Alaska and northern British Columbia were undreamt of not so many years back, and the Alaskan grizzly is, too, I believe, a new species.

It is, therefore, far from unreasonable to believe or to hope that as the country is opened up the fisherman will also achieve new conquests. As yet they lie before him, for he only follows slowly in the footsteps of the pioneer and the big-game hunter; he requires a railway and an hotel, and he must be able to dispose in some manner of his catch, which he cannot do unless he is at least near some settlement. I have conversed with numbers of prospectors and hunters from all parts of the north-west, and they all have the same account of teeming rivers and lakes. Many a weird fish story have they told me, but none have really been fishermen; they have simply caught fish for food, and have not noted them much except with a view to their edible properties. It is, therefore, highly probable that, as these strange waters are gradually made accessible to the angler and become as well known as the more southern rivers of British Columbia, many interesting facts will become known too, and new varieties of trout and other fish will be discovered. Even those southern waters are, in truth, little known, and several interesting matters which could well bear investigation will be put forward in these pages.

CHAPTER II.

Season for Trout Fishing—Principal Districts—Tackle Necessary—"No Drawing-room Work"—Advantage of Plenty of Time—Poor Fishing in the Rockies—The Thompson River—The South Thompson—Its Course and Character—Clear, Swift Water—Difficulty of Landing Big Fish—A Lost Thirty-pounder—The Successful Cherokee Fisherman—Fine, Calm Days Best for Fishing—Mosquitoes not Troublesome.

FLY-FISHING for trout in British Columbia may be said to begin in April or May at the coast, but in the interior it is June or July before much success can be obtained. If time be no object, good sport might be obtained in the coast rivers and lakes during April and May, and a move might be made to the interior waters during June and July, while August is about the best season for the big salmon fishing on Vancouver Island. During September and October good sport may still be obtained, and the fish are then in the best condition; but usually the attractions of shooting prove too much for the local sportsman, and the rivers are more or less deserted. The southern waters may be divided into three principal districts

—namely, the coast rivers, the Thompson River district, and the waters of the Kootenay country, which all seem to possess special peculiarities, though the rainbow is found in them all. But in the coast rivers the steelhead, or sea-trout, is alone met with.

As regards rods and tackle for trout fishing, large rods are out of place in British Columbia, and quite unnecessary; an 11ft. split cane is the best, and long enough for any river; a 14ft. rod is very unhandy in a rough country or among trees, and all local fishermen use a small rod. Tackle should be of the same kind as one would use for sea-trout fishing, and should be strong. As regards flies, size is the most important consideration, as the usual patterns are the ordinary sea-trout and loch flies. The imitation stone fly is about the only fly that should resemble the natural insect. Rather large flies are used on the rivers, and smaller on the lakes, but this question may be left till individual streams are described. For a general supply large sea-trout flies (Jock Scott, Silver Grey, and Silver Doctor, etc.), with some March Browns and stone flies of the same sizes, and an assortment of smaller Scottish loch trout flies of various patterns—these are all that are needed. The artificial minnow of various kinds, the spoon, and the dead bait on a crocodile or Archer spinner are all used, and the prawn has lately been tried with deadly effect on large fish. Bottles of preserved minnows and small prawns would therefore be a useful addition to the equipment. It is also wise to take plenty of strong casts and traces, as local fishing tackle is not to be trusted.

It must be noted well that fishing in these waters is no drawing-room work; great sport can be got, but the best is often only to be obtained by a certain amount of "roughing it." The rivers are not always in right condition, nor the weather always favourable—unfortunate facts peculiar to every river in the world—and it is only when all things are favourable that the best sport is obtained. To have plenty of time at his disposal is the great thing for the fisherman, for it is only natural that a man passing through the country and having only a couple of weeks at the outside to spare may easily find nothing but disappointments. No one must expect to get off the Canadian Pacific express and find the rainbow trout eagerly expecting his arrival.

The district best known to me is that through which the Thompson River runs, from the Shuswap Lake to its junction with the Fraser at Lytton. The Canadian Pacific Railway follows the river in its whole length, and thus renders it very accessible. Many other smaller streams and lakes are part of the Thompson water system, and afford good fishing. The river runs through the "dry belt," which is so called owing to the smallness of the rainfall, which only averages about 8in. in the year. It is from this cause that the banks of the rivers are very open and free from brush, which makes them easy to fish and to travel along; while, for the same reason, the country is generally open rolling hills, covered with grass or scanty pines, affording a great contrast to the moist country at the coast, where the rivers run through thick woods and impenetrable bush, which render them very difficult to approach and fish unless they are shallow enough for wading The fishing to be obtained along the Canadian Pacific Railway as it passes through the Rocky Mountains is not very good, the guide-books notwithstanding. At Banff there is a little fishing in the Bow River, but it is poor, and the fish do not seem to take the fly. In Devil's Lake lake trout, a species of char, can be got on the spoon by deep trolling up to a very large size; but it is not a very high form of sport, and cannot be compared to the rainbow trout fishing along the Thompson.

The South Thompson River has its source at

the western end of the great Shuswap Lake, near Shuswap station on the Canadian Pacific, and joins the Fraser at Lytton; at Kamloops it is joined by the North Thompson, and the combined stream flows into Kamloops Lake, about seven miles below the town, running out again some twenty miles below at Savona's Ferry. Its total course being about 140 miles, and almost all of it fishing water, it is a fine river. The water is usually clear, varying in breadth and in swiftness of current according to the nature of the country it flows through. In places it is broad and calm; in the canyons it is a rushing torrent. Its pace below Savona's is from eight to twelve miles an hour, above Kamloops probably not more than two to four. The South Thompson from Shuswap Lake to Kamloops is always clear, owing to the filtration of the lake, and fine fishing can be had in some of the upper rapids and pools. Near Kamloops the current is too sluggish, and sport is not very good. The river flows along the South Thompson valley, an open country with scattered farms and cattle ranches, bordered by bunch grass range and hills covered by yellow pine, very beautiful in spring and early summer. It is the central plateau of British Columbia, and has an exceedingly dry climate, with hardly any rain, very healthy and bracing, the altitude being about 1200ft above sea level; it is very hot in summer, and sometimes cold in winter. Fishing begins here early in June, and, though it is little fished, there is no better part of the river. In Kamloops Lake the rainbow is very plentiful, and good fishing may be obtained as early as June at Tranquille, where the river flows into the lake, and causes a slow, wide-sweeping eddy. From Savona's Ferry, the outflow of the lake, down to Ashcroft is the best-known part of the river, and here the current is very swift and the banks are rocky and steep. Near Lytton the canyon is so deep and the banks so steep and dangerous that fishing is out of the question.

On the whole there is probably no fishing river in British Columbia to beat this one for the size and quality of the fish, though it does not afford the large bags that can be obtained on the Kootenay. It is a very sporting river, owing to the strength of the current, for a big fish is hard to hold if it once gets out into the main current, away from the side eddies. Mainly owing to this is the fact that there seems to be no record of fish over about 4lb., for a larger fish can get into the main stream, where the force of a ten-mile current drags on it and the line to such an extent that there is no chance of holding it. Such large fish are rarely met with, but every fisherman on the Thompson has stories of them, and they are all the same and coincide with my own. It was only once my luck to hook a really large fish. He jumped out of the water twice close to me, and I had a splendid view of him, and judged him to be about 8lb. He headed for the opposite bank, and just as a break was inevitable the fly came back. Other men have told me the same story, but such large fish are hooked so seldom that it is not worth while using a stronger rod and tackle. Though very large fish are undoubtedly plentiful, they seldom take either fly or any other bait, and perhaps deep live baiting would be the only means of successfully fishing for them.

The average fish is from $\frac{1}{2}$lb. to 4lb., but much larger fish are in the deep pools I once was shown at Spence's Bridge three supposed salmon in the winter which had been speared and sold by the Indians for two shillings apiece. I noticed their perfect condition and bright red side stripe, and, on examining them more carefully, pointed out to an experienced fisherman who was present, and to the proprietor of the hotel and others, that these fish were large rainbow trout. The largest weighed 15lb., the two others 12lb. apiece. This incident happened at Spence's Bridge, on the Lower Thompson. On another occasion of a visit there, the bar-tender of the hotel, who happened to be a young Englishman, told me that the angling editor of an American sporting paper had stayed off there and proposed to try with spoon and minnow for large rainbow trout, which he had heard could be got. The next day they went to where the Nicola River, a large stream, flows into the Thompson about half a mile from the hotel The angling editor was provided with strong spinning gear and rod, and much to the bar-tender's surprise, very soon got into a fish of most surprising strength and dimensions, for they saw him several times, and estimated him at the unbelievable weight of over 30lb. The fish took them rapidly down to some impassable rocks, and went away with everything but the rod. I believed this story at the time, and see no reason to disbelieve now, though of course the size of the fish was probably overestimated No other fish was seen or hooked. The only point which I would wish to call attention to is the probable great size of the rainbows in this river, though none have as yet been taken with the rod. Mr. Langley's fish of 22lb. proves that in the lakes these large fish exist. At this place Mr. Inskip has also caught some large fish by spinning, and some very good bags of smaller fish have been got on the fly.

The Thompson is not very much fished. Near Ashcroft the local sportsmen from that small town fish it, and Savona's Ferry is visited from Kamloops when the fish are taking; but Kamloops Lake must provide an inexhaustible reserve of fish to take the place of fish caught, so that the river could never be really fished out or much overfished under present conditions. The Indians also fish, and generally with the illegal salmon roe, but do not make great catches; the fly is more successful when the fish are taking it. Nets and dynamite would be useless in this river; therefore, even should a far greater population inhabit the surrounding country, which is not likely for a great number of years, this beautiful and striking river will still afford great sport for many generations. There are long stretches which are never touched except by a stray Indian or Chinaman with a grasshopper or bit of salmon roe on a string tied to a long willow pole. Some years ago a nondescript individual who said he was a Cherokee half-breed turned up at Savona's Ferry and earned a living by fishing. Every day he caught more fish than he could carry, though he never revealed his secret. Some believed that he used set lines.

His success showed that trout were far more numerous than was generally believed, but the fly fishermen caught as many as usual. He was the most successful fisherman I ever saw.

It is a fact very striking to the English fisherman that the best fishing days in British Columbia are the exact opposite of ours. Fine, bright hot days without wind are the best, both on river and lake, cold and rainy days are always bad, a fortunate thing, as such days are very uncommon. Strong wind is, oddly enough, the greatest enemy of the angler, especially on the lakes; it nearly always puts the fish down. The only thing that seems to account for these curious facts is the probability that the stone fly and other flies are not hatched out except on hot days, while the fish are regardless of the gleam of the gut in the water. My own experience has always been that the hottest days are the best. Except for rocks and stones, and clambering up and down very steep banks, the Thompson River is easy to fish, and trees are not troublesome. Mosquitoes are almost absent, except in the south branch, and the Canadian Pacific, as has been said, runs along its whole length, thus giving easy access to the river, while hotels exist at most of the stations. The railway company publishes a pamphlet on shooting and fishing, but the Thompson River is altogether omitted, which is certainly very strange, as the line runs along the banks for its whole distance, and there is no part of British Columbia in which such excellent fishing can be obtained, and no part of Canada which enjoys such a climate or offers such strangely attractive scenery.

CHAPTER III.

The Kamloops District—Kamloops as Headquarters—May Floods and Fishing in Shuswap Lake—Silver-bodied Flies—Streams Running into the Lake—The Eagle River—Advantages of a Steam Launch—A Big Catch—Possibilities of the Prawn—A July Spectacle—Fishing at Tranquille—Kamloops Lake—Savona's Ferry—Great Sport in June—Dolly Varden Trout—A Fifteen-Pounder—Falling-off of Sport when Salmon are Running—The "Salmon Fly"—Size of Catches on the Thompson—August a Bad Month.

THE Thompson district may be described for fishing purposes as beginning at Sicamous junction and ending a little below Spence's Bridge, including the Shuswap and Okanagan lakes, Kamloops Nicola, and Mammit lakes, and the mountain lakes in the neighbourhood, all of which are more or less part of the Thompson watershed. Of this country the town of Kamloops is the centre, situated at the junction of the north and south branches of the river, and seven miles above Kamloops Lake, its name meaning, in the Thompson language, "the meeting of the waters." By virtue of its position it is an excellent headquarters for anyone wishing to fish in the district, for by rail, stage, or horseback every portion of it can be reached from there, and there are good stores to outfit from, and good hotels—for British Columbia. Fishing in this district cannot be said really to begin till May is well advanced. It is when the snow begins to melt in earnest and the rivers and creeks come down in flood that real sport commences, and this usually happens towards the end of May. No sport can be obtained in the Thompson River below Kamloops Lake at this time, as the water is discoloured by the North Thompson flowing in at Kamloops, which makes fishing useless, and it is only in the South Thompson and the Shuswap Lake that good sport can be obtained.

As the rivers begin to come down in high flood the trout congregate at the places where the streams flow into the Shuswap Lake, doubtless for the food which is brought down, and after two or three hot days, when these small mountain streams rise rapidly, fishing is always good. The fish may be seen leaping and splashing in great numbers at the place where the turbid waters of the stream mingle with the clear water of the lake. Small fry are the object of their pursuit, and if a silver-bodied fly is thrown over a moving fish he takes it with a rush almost without fail. It is a most exciting form of fishing, for the fly must be thrown quickly from a boat or canoe over the fish as he breaks the water in his rush for the minnows, and if he fails to see it further casting is often useless, till another fish repeats the same manœuvre. It would seem as if the trout were lying in wait till a small school of young salmon or trout became entangled in the strong eddies of the stream, darting out upon them when thus comparatively helpless. An occasional fish may be got by casting here and there over the water, but it is only when the trout are moving on the surface that really good sport can be obtained.

All the Shuswap mountain creeks and rivers during late May and in June and July give opportunities for good fishing of this kind. The Eagle River, about a quarter of a mile from Sicamous, is a good example; and there are numerous other streams at various points in the Shuswap Lake (some probably almost unknown) which can be fished at this time of the year. I remember a bag of 80lb of fish taken on the fly at the mouth of Eagle River some few years ago in three hours' fishing; but it has not been equalled lately, though there is no reason why it should not be, in favourable circumstances. The time to look for is when the first flood comes down the Eagle River after two or three hot days, and there must not be any wind to speak of on the lake. The fish may be seen leaping, from the hotel windows, and it is then that the fisherman must row his fastest to the mouth of the river, and if they are still moving when he gets there his success is assured. The best way to enjoy sport on the Shuswap Lake is to hire a steam launch and cruise round to the mouths of the various streams and try them in turn. Anasty Arm, Scotch, and Adam's Creek are the best known. A canoe or boat must be taken to fish from, and unless sleeping accommodation can be got on the boat, it is necessary to camp on the shore. If a steam launch is beyond the fisherman's means, the only other way is to hire a boat, with an Indian or other guide, and carry a tent and provisions Wood and water are plentiful, and there is only one objection to the plan, that the mosquito is often very numerous and troublesome on the Shuswap, and Sicamous is by no means exempt. If, however, the sportsman can sleep on a steam launch, this nuisance is got rid of, as it is only on the shore that the mosquito is plentiful. No more pleasant or sporting trip could well be undertaken than one in the Shuswap Lake from Sicamous in June, with a suitable steamer or launch, for great fishing, both with fly and troll, would be certain at the mouths of all the creeks and rivers; and if a rifle were taken, bear, both black and grizzly, are by no means uncommon.

There is also another place, hitherto little fished except by the Indians, which is well worthy of a trial. It is in the centre of the lake, where the four arms meet, a place well known to the men who log on the lake. It takes the form of a channel less than half a mile wide, connecting the four arms of the Shuswap Lake. Here in 1903, in early August, two men camped, going up on a logging steamer from Kamloops. They trolled across and across the channel, and caught in about ten days some thirty large silver fish, the biggest being about 15lb. Many were lost including one monster supposed to be about 25lb. The best day's sport was about eight large fish. I do not know whether this place has ever been fished since, but it certainly deserves a trial. At the mouths of the various creeks I have never heard definitely of anything over 7lb. being caught but the fish are always in splendid condition and give a great display of fight. The best flies are those with silver bodies, such as the Silver Doctor, Silver Grey, and Wilkinson. A dead bait on an archer spinner is very deadly, and the abylone spoon; a half-red spoon is to be avoided, or a half-gold. A large species of char may be caught by deep trolling with a weight and spoon; but it is a poor kind of sport, and the fish is not game. The prawn has never been tried on the Shuswap Lake; it might be worth a trial. Large trout have been taken on the prawn in the coast rivers; but it is possible that they were sea-trout and not rainbows.

The upper part of the South Thompson, for a mile or more after it leaves the Shuswap, is good at the same time of the year in certain pools and eddies, or riffles as they are called locally. I once, in early July, saw a wonderful sight on this part of the river, at a place called Sullivan's Pool. I was passing in a logging steamer on a very hot morning, and in a back eddy which forms this pool, under a cut bank, the water was alive with large trout chasing the small fry on the surface. As each fish drove the little fish upwards a band of about thirty mergansers attacked them from above A curious and very lively scene was the result, such as I have never seen before or since. On returning about seven in the evening, at my request the steamer was tied up to the bank, and I put out in a small boat with a boatman, though no fish were stirring and the mergansers were sitting gorged in a row on the bank. However, I hooked and landed at the first cast a beautiful 4½lb. rainbow, which was promptly cooked for dinner. If it had been possible to fish the pool in the morning a great catch could have been made At this time of the year good fishing can be got at Tranquille, where the river flows into Kamloops Lake and forms a slow-moving eddy. Fishing is the same here as in the Shuswap; it is only good on hot, calm days, and wind puts the fish down. It is best when the fish can be seen splashing on the surface in the early morning or evening, when good catches of fine fish may be made; but, as wind is by no means uncommon, it is not always that circumstances are favourable

Tranquille is seven miles from Kamloops, on the other side of the river, and comfortable accommodation can be got at Mr Fortune's ranch It is a beautiful place, but mosquitoes are not unknown Here Capt. Drummond landed a 12½lb. fish on the fly, and a model cut out in wood was preserved for a long time, but was burnt in a fire that took place there some few years ago. This is the largest rainbow caught on the fly that I have ever heard of. In May and June, before the fish will take the fly, there is often fair sport to be had with the minnow and spoon in Kamloops Lake; unless the north branch of the Thompson is in very high flood and discolours the water too much. The north branch, which joins the South Thompson at Kamloops, is no good for fishing; its waters are seldom clear enough, and seem to be fed too much by glaciers, with no large lake to clear and filter the water. There are several rivers of the same type in British Columbia, and fishing does not seem to be good in any of them. At the western end of Kamloops Lake the Thompson flows out again to join the Fraser at Lytton; the stream is swift and strong, running when in high flood at the rate of twelve miles an hour. In 1894 there was a very high water, and the stationmaster at Savona's wired to Ashcroft, a distance of twenty-four miles, to say that the bridge had just been carried away A reply came giving the time of its arrival, which was just two hours afterwards. The *débris* swept away the Ashcroft bridge and also the bridge at Lytton.

At Savona's the fishing of the Lower Thompson begins, and at this point, about a mile from the mouth of the river, there is an excellent hotel, kept by Mr. Adam Fergusson, one of the "old timers" of British Columbia, who came into the country with many others in the early days of the gold diggings on the Fraser River. This is really the only fishing hotel on the upper mainland of British

Columbia, and is an excellent headquarters from which several lakes can be reached, as also many places on each side of the Thompson River This part of the Thompson River affords good fishing from Savona's to below Spence's bridge, wherever the water is accessible, and, though a little sport can be obtained in the latter part of May, chiefly with spoon and minnow, it is not usually till July that the river is in really good order, when the excess of snow water has been carried off and the river begins to fall and get clearer. The hot weather sets in at the beginning of June, and a quick rise of the river is an immediate result. On a rising water the trout will not take. Often there is a pronounced fall in the middle of June, owing to cooler weather setting in, though this does not always happen. When it does occur excellent fishing can be obtained. I remember its happening in the middle of June, 1901, and for a week there was tremendous sport; a trout rose to every cast of the fly; but as soon as the water began to rise again everything was at an end.

At the end of May, before the water begins to rise, a fair number of fish can be taken by spinning from the bank with spoon and minnow at the mouth of the river. But these are another fish, called locally the Dolly Varden trout, a species of char, a handsome fish with pink spots and light pink flesh, and good eating. They take the fly later on occasionally, and run from $\frac{3}{4}$lb to 4lb., but are not so lively as the rainbow, though they are a strong and game fish. I once took fifteen in a day's fishing with the minnow, and they can also be caught by trolling from a boat near the mouth of the river, the sport being varied by an occasional rainbow, often of a larger size than those usually caught with the fly. In May, 1903, a Dolly Varden of 15lb. was taken. It is a curious fact that during the fly season in July very few of these fish are ever taken, either on fly or spoon, or by trolling in the lake.

The fly-fishing season at Savona's really begins about the first of July and lasts till the salmon first arrive in the beginning of August, when fishing invariably falls off, probably owing to the fact that the trout follow the salmon to their spawning beds to prey on the eggs; at least, such is the local reason given. Whether this is true or not it is impossible to say, but in any case the fact remains that about this time fly fishing falls off for a few weeks coincident with the appearance of the salmon, and generally is poor during the whole of August, at any rate at Savona's. (It is often as good as ever lower down the river.) If a grasshopper is used some fish may still be caught, especially if the bait be allowed to sink. Later on, at the beginning of September, the fish will again take the fly and continue to do so until the end of the season, about the middle of October, while I have been told by an ardent fisherman that he had excellent sport in November during a snowstorm, regardless of the law of British Columbia. The excellence of sport in July depends a good deal on the rise of the stone fly, or " salmon fly " as it is locally called, and it is not until this fly makes its appearance that fishing becomes really good.

This insect in appearance is the same as the English stone fly, but is much more plentiful on the Thompson than I have ever seen it elsewhere, in some seasons every bush on the bank is literally covered with the flies, and later on the rocks are strewn with their dead bodies. A good stone fly season is always a good fishing season, for the fish are clearly very fond of them, and may often be seen sucking them into their mouths as fast as they fall into the water, or jumping at them as they dip down to the river's surface to lay their eggs. I have often seen the salmon fly become suddenly very numerous about mid-day or an hour or so before that, the hot sun hatching them out, and at once the trout are on the move, readily taking a fly tied to imitate the natural one, and continuing to do so as long as the living fly is on the water. At this time the best hours for fishing are the middle ones of the day, however hot and bright they may be, for in the earlier and later hours the fly is not on the water. I have never found, as a rule, that very late or very early hours are favourable on this river during this month, except just at the place where the river leaves the lake, which is usually good in the evening, especially after a very hot day. The best fly at this time is one tied to resemble as nearly as possible the living salmon fly; but if the natural fly is not on the water, others may be tried, such as the Jock Scott, the Silver Doctor, Wilkinson, March Brown and other well-known flies. Some local men swear by a claret body, others prefer a yellow or green; but, whatever fly is used, I believe that it should have plenty of hackle and body, and be of good size (Nos. 4 and 5); small flies are not advisable.

Great bags must not, as a rule, be expected on the Thompson; fifteen to twenty good fish is an excellent bag on this river. Mr. F. J. Fulton, of Kamloops, who has fished this river more than anyone else, has never done better than twenty-four fish, but these twenty-four fish would be 48lb., and ought to include at least a couple of fish about 4lb. apiece. On the Thompson the angler must carry his own fish, besides climbing up and down some very steep banks under the glare of a northern sun, whose heat is increased tenfold by the water and the bare rocks. Such a day's fishing is no mean trial of endurance, while the fierceness of the stream will generally account for a good percentage of lost fish. With regard to the falling off of sport in August, it may be quite possible that the salmon may really have nothing to do with the poorness of fishing at this time, but that the real reason may be that the fish are fat and gorged with the abundance of fly and grasshopper, and lie lazily, deep in the pools. In other parts of British Columbia fishing is poor at this time, and in waters the salmon cannot reach. And this reasoning is rather borne out by the fact that towards the end of August or beginning of September the fish begin to take again, though the salmon are still running in vast numbers. One of the best catches I ever saw taken from the Thompson (thirty-six fish) was got in early October, and the trout rose up among the travelling masses of salmon and took the fly.

Every part of the Thompson is fishable to below Spence's Bridge, over forty miles from Savona's, and the fishing is often irregular, by which is meant that when sport is good at Ashcroft it is not very good at Savona's, and *vice versá*. I have known the fish to be entirely off at the mouth of the river near Savona's, while good bags have been got a few miles below. This will show that sport on this part of the Thompson is somewhat variable; but still one point may be emphasised, namely, that during the two months of July and August there is always good fishing to be obtained at one point or another along the river, and all can be easily reached from the Savona's Hotel. The southern bank is followed by the main line of the Canadian Pacific Railway, and is therefore easy of access; the northern bank can only be reached on foot or on horseback, and is therefore not so much fished. To fish this bank far down it would be necessary to seek hospitality for a night or two from some rancher.

CHAPTER IV.

What is the "Silver Trout"?—Evidence in Favour of a New Species—Difference in Appearance from the Rainbow—A Jumper—Native of Kamloops and Shuswap Lakes—A Bag of Twenty-four—The Dolly Varden—Origin of the Name—Not a Free Riser—Grayling—Chub and Squaw Fish—Great Lake Trout—The Silver Fish at Spence's Bridge—Salmon or Steelhead?—Cut-throat Trout—Possible Fishing Tour in British Columbia.

IT still remains a question, which has never yet been decided, whether there are not two distinct species of trout in these waters. There is no question that locally such is universally thought to be the case. Every local fisherman speaks of having caught a red side or a silver trout, and firmly believes that they are distinct species. Should this be really the case, it is a matter of no little interest, as a new and very beautiful species would be added to those already known and described. A brief account of the evidence, for and against, may not be out of place, and might result in some final conclusion being arrived at For several years two Americans came every season to Savona's Ferry to fish, and, becoming impressed with the beauty of the so-called silver trout, they sent a specimen to Professor Starr Jordan, of the Leland Stanford University of San Francisco. The first specimen did not arrive in good condition, and another specimen was sent, in the preparation of which I personally assisted. It was a fish of about 1½lb. in weight, a very beautiful specimen and a most typical example of the silver trout

Professor Jordan described this fish as a new species, under the name of *Salmo kamloopsii*, and he so describes it in a monograph on the salmon and trout of the Pacific Coast, published by the State Board of Fisheries for the State of California. In this account he gives expert reasons, founded on the number of rays in the anal fin and tail, the position of the opercula, and the size of the body scales, suggesting, moreover, that the fish might turn out to be a connecting link between the true salmonidæ and the genus oncorhynchus or Pacific Coast salmon. He suggested that a further specimen should be sent, in order that the intestinal tract might be examined; but this suggestion was unfortunately not complied with. I am not prepared to say whether Professor Jordan still adheres to this opinion, or whether the silver trout has been fully recognised among ichthyologists as a distinct species. In a recent letter to me, however, he states that he considers the Kamloops trout to be "only a slight variation of the steelhead," which statement shows that its exact identity is not established, for the steelhead is absolutely unknown in these upper waters, and the silver trout never goes down to the sea. To the best of my belief it is a fact that no further specimens have been examined by any naturalist of note, and the question is therefore still *in statu quo*. It is a matter, I would humbly suggest, that is well worthy of solution. So far as I am aware, Professor Jordan is the only expert who has examined this fish. The only other evidence as to its existence as a distinct species is the widespread local opinion, which is also held by the half-breeds and Indians, who undoubtedly believe that there are two kinds of trout in the Thompson River. Such evidence or belief is not scientific proof, but is certainly of considerable weight, until it is proved to be mistaken.

I have always been firmly convinced that the two fish are perfectly distinct, and this opinion is fully shared by all the local anglers. If two well-marked specimens are seen side by side the difference in appearance is most remarkable. The silver trout is less heavily built, the head is smaller and sharper, the scales are smaller in size, and the stripe on the side is violet instead of pink. There is only one alternative opinion, namely, that for an unknown reason some rainbows acquire this peculiar silvery appearance. Whatever may be the final decision, the fact still remains, that a fish of a different type from the ordinary rainbow is common in these waters, and is well deserving of a description. The back is green, with the usual black spots, the sides and belly of a bright silver, like a fresh-run salmon, but instead of the pink or crimson stripe of the rainbow there is a similar band of a delicate violet or purple hue. If two well-marked specimens are laid side by side the difference is most marked, though difficult to describe exactly The silver trout is a cleaner-cut fish, and looks exactly as if it had come straight from salt water; one would hardly feel surprised to see the sea lice sticking to its sides.

From a fisherman's point of view it is gamer, and is always out of the water when hooked, appearing also to be more addicted to taking silver-bodied flies, being more of a small fry than a fly feeder. It is usually caught at the mouths of streams running into the large lakes, and at the outflow of the Thompson at Savona's, where it can be seen chasing the small fry on the surface. It must, however, be admitted that some local anglers consider it to be merely the rainbow when in the pink of condition, with the colour simply modified by the clear waters of the lakes, and there is, moreover, no doubt that the poorer the condition of the rainbow the deeper is the red of its stripe, though, on the other hand, I have seen splendid fish in which the stripe was very deep crimson. Spent fish, however, have always a deep red stripe.

This silvery fish seems to be chiefly native to the Kamloops and Shuswap lakes, whence it spreads into the Thompson It appears to be much less common in the river than in the lake waters, except just at the outflow near Savona's, which is a favourite resort, where in warm evenings in July and August it may be seen chasing the minnows in the first pool A few years ago I made a bag of twenty-four fish, weighing 48lb , in two evenings between the hours of seven and eight; four of these fish weighed 4lb. apiece. The fishing here must be done from a boat, as the eddy where they move is beyond the reach of the bank It is a most exciting kind of fishing, as it is almost useless to cast except over a moving fish; the pool is still for some minutes, and then, in a moment, a dozen or more fish will be at the surface rushing among the small fry, who leap out of the water to escape them. If a silver-bodied fly be thrown over one of these fish he is certain to take it, and if two flies are used the second fly is certain to be seized as well, while, owing to the strong water, a desperate fight is the result, and the strongest single-gut is often broken. But it is by no means on every evening that this sport can be enjoyed, and in some seasons the fish are much more plentiful in this pool than others. It must also be in hot, still weather, as a wind always puts them down. The fishing obviously depends on the presence of the shoals of small fish, probably young salmon. The silver trout lie in wait for them here, and when a shoal is entangled in the strong eddy they rush upon them. This is the same form of sport which can be enjoyed at the mouth of the streams which run into the Shuswap Lake, the Eagle River at Sicamous, and Scotch and Adams Creeks In connection with this fish it is worthy of note that the rainbow is a species which shows little tendency to vary from the type. I have caught them in a great number of the streams and lakes of this district, and they never seem to vary in the least. A specimen from one lake could not be distinguished from any other; they are always typical rainbows with the red stripe, and no silvery fish are ever seen, unless the lake is directly connected with the Thompson River. Thus the silver form is found in Shuswap, Kamloops, and Nicola lakes, but in the large mountain lakes which have no open communication with the river only the ordinary rainbow is found. There is only one exception, the Long Lake near Vernon, which contains a beautiful silvery fish, to be alluded to later. This lake is, I believe, indirectly connected with the Shuswap.

There are other interesting fish found in the Thompson and the Kamloops and Shuswap lakes, but they are not of much use to the fisherman, though occasionally caught. The Dolly Varden trout, a species of char, has been alluded to, and is the only one which affords much sport to the fisherman; it runs to a large size, as has been stated, but does not often take the fly. Its curious name is said to be derived indirectly from Dickens and the time of his tours in the United States, which produced a Dolly Varden craze in hats and some kinds of calico patterns, of which one with pink spots was supposed to be the correct Dolly Varden pattern. On seeing this fish for the first time, some young lady is supposed to have exclaimed that it was a "Dolly Varden trout," and the name appears to have been generally adopted.

However this may be, there is no other name for the fish except its scientific one, and it is known all through the West as the Dolly Varden trout.

It is strong and game, but not so lively as a trout. It takes the fly very seldom, and then generally only when about a pound or less in weight. On the other hand, in May it takes the minnow and spoon quite readily. Later on, in July and after, it is rarely that one is caught. I once caught two of 4lb. and 5lb. on a fly in July, the only ones so caught during that month, and have landed many on minnow and spoon. That it reaches a large size is proved by the capture of the fish alluded to above, which weighed 15lb. The man who caught it informed me that it was got on the fly, and I was never able to find out the true history of its capture, but strongly suspect it was lured to its doom by a piece of raw beef. The Dolly Varden is a greyish-coloured fish with light salmon-coloured spots of rather a large size.

An occasional grayling is caught on the fly, but they are not plentiful. I have never seen one over 2lb. A small fish, like a grayling, but without any adipose fin, sometimes takes the fly; it has a bright orange tinge on its side, and has white flesh, which is firm and very good eating. The chub is very common, and will take the fly, but is regarded as vermin, being very poor eating; it runs up to 4lb. and over. The squaw fish, also, will take the fly sometimes, but more often the minnow or grasshopper, its flesh is white and tasteless. It is a large-mouthed fish greatly resembling the chub and attaining about the same size. Both chub and squaw fish are great devourers of fry. In the Shuswap Lake, by trolling in deep water with a lead attached, a large grey char with pink spots can be caught, running up to perhaps 20lb, and being usually known as the lake trout or great lake trout; it takes a spoon, but is very sluggish, and does not give any real sport. The Indians catch these fish. I have never heard of their being caught in Kamloops Lake. With reference to the run of Pacific salmon, it is interesting to note that large silvery fish have been caught by minnow and spoon in the Shuswap Lake, notably in the narrow strait mentioned above. Mr. Inskip has within the last year or two written some letters to the *Field* describing the capture of a number of silver fish up to 10lb weight near Spence's Bridge, at the mouth of the Nicola river, where it joins the Thompson. He believes these fish to be salmon, and it is possible that his view may be correct. But it is also possible that they may be silver trout or steelhead trout, the evidence is not yet complete. No salmon have ever been taken in this way with spoon or minnow above this point, in spite of the number of years that fishing has been carried on in these waters. The Indians never catch salmon by trolling with the spoon, though they troll persistently for trout, the line being fastened to the paddle of their canoe.

Mr. Inskip states that these fish never take the fly, and he has only caught them in October. There is, of course, no doubt of the truth of his statement, and a possible explanation might be that the steelheads run up as far as this point, and go up to the Nicola River. It has never been thought that the steelhead runs as far as Kamloops Lake, and I have never heard of anyone who claimed to have caught one; it is, however, quite within the bounds of possibility that some of these fish may come up with the salmon. The problem can be easily solved by counting the rays in the anal fin; in the true trout these rays only amount to about nine, in the salmon there are fourteen to sixteen well-developed rays.

The cut-throat trout is unknown to me. I have never caught it in British Columbian waters, unless some fish mentioned later in the account of the Nicola River belonged to this species. It may occur in some of the southern British Columbian coast rivers, and is common further south in the neighbouring States of the Union. Prof. Jordan states that it is always found in the country of the Sioux Indians, and hazards a suggestion that they may have taken their tribal mark from it. This mark consists of a couple of lines of red paint under the jaw on each side of the neck, and is very similar to that which gives this fish its curious name. The rainbow and the so-called silver trout are the only kinds which are met with in the central plateau of British Columbia.

The next subject for consideration will be the fishing in the mountain lakes; but before proceeding to it it may be as well to consider the fishing as a whole in the waters already described, for the question which most naturally suggests itself to an Englishman is whether the sport to be obtained is worth coming so far for. Anyone with the necessary money and time at his disposal might prefer Norway or Scotland. It would certainly not be worth anybody's while to come such a distance to enjoy the two or three weeks at Savona's, which represent, at the outside, the time of the best fishing on the Lower Thompson. It would be necessary for the fisherman to have plenty of time at his disposal, so as to visit the different places at the time when the fishing was respectively at its best. Thus June could be spent in trying the sport on the Shuswap Lake, with Sicamous as headquarters, while a visit could be paid from there to the Okanagan Lakes, which can be easily reached in three hours by rail. In July the Lower Thompson can be fished from Savona's as a headquarters, while from there several lakes can be tried during July and August, the trip being concluded by a visit to the salmon rivers of the coast during late August and early September. After that time big game or duck shooting might he tried. The time mentioned would also allow for a visit to the fishing on the Kootenay River near Nelson. There is hardly any need to say that all fishing in British Columbia is free to everyone, and, although there is a little more fishing done than a few years ago, no one need be afraid of overfishing. There is plenty of room, and there will continue to be so for a very long time yet, except in a neighbourhood close to any very large town. The fishing in waters hitherto described may be compared, in my opinion, to very good sea-trout fishing, which it closely resembles. As stated before, sport depends, as in every country, on certain states of water and weather. A great bag cannot be an everyday occurrence, but if the right places are visited at the right time there is great sport to be obtained.

CHAPTER V.

Other Lakes—Long Lake—Its Silvery Trout—Fish Lake—
Extraordinary Fishing—Fifteen Hundred Trout in Three
Days—A Miniature Gaff—Uses of a Collapsible Boat—
Catching Fish Through the Ice—Mammit Lake—Nicola
Lake—Beautifully Marked Trout in Nicola River—"The
Little Red Fish."

THE Thompson and its two great lakes, the Kamloops and Shuswap, having been dealt with, the fishing in the mountain lakes remains to be described. The sport to be obtained in some of these waters must be somewhat unique, for though I believe it is surpassed in size of fish by some of the New Zealand lakes, it is impossible that it can be surpassed anywhere in the weight and number of fish captured in one day's fishing. There are great numbers of lakes far back in the mountains in which no fishing has ever been done, and others there are in which no one but a stray prospector, hunter, or Indian has ever thrown a line; but these, of course, need not be considered. There are a good number which have had their capabilities tested, and are locally more or less well known. The chief fishing lakes in this district are the Nicola and Okanagan lakes, which are very large, and the smaller ones Fish and Mammit, together with numerous smaller lakes which are less known. In the Okanagan district, near the little town of Vernon, there is a beautiful piece of water called Long Lake, about sixteen miles long by less than a mile wide, about four miles from the town. The water is very clear and the lake very deep, the cliffs on each side running down sheer into the water. The trout in this lake are remarkable for their size and extreme beauty; the rainbow characteristic is entirely absent, for they are of a pure silver colour, with the merest trace of a pink tinge along the side; they resemble, in fact, a fresh-run grilse straight from the sea, and no fish which could be called a rainbow is ever caught. The fish run to a large size, 5lb. being by no means uncommon, and fish from this weight up to 12lb. have been often caught. These large fish are caught by trolling in the ordinary way with spoon and minnow, for the fly fishing is very uncertain. There appear to be certain places along the sides of the lake to which the fish come up from the deep water on the look out for fly food, but on the whole it is a trolling lake, and differs in this respect from almost all the other lakes to be mentioned. It may be that these fish are the same as the specimen described by Professor Jordan, and are really a distinct species, feeding mainly on small fry, and not much addicted to a fly diet. In appearance they certainly deserve the name of silver trout. I am not aware that any specimen has ever been examined by any scientific authority on fish.

I fished once in July on this lake, and caught two fish about 1½lb. apiece on the fly, while another of about 3lb. was taken on a minnow. Dr. Gerald Williams, of Vernon, fishes here a great deal, and gave me the above information. He prefers this lake to the neighbouring Okanagan Lake, but stated that the same fish were to be found in both This lake seems well worth a visit, for if only a few fish were the result of a day's work their beauty and possible size would be worth the trouble, while the lake and its scenery are characteristic of the most beautiful part of the interior of British Columbia, surrounded as it is by rolling hills of bunch grass, range, and pine-covered bluffs Vernon can be easily reached by train from Sicamous, on the Canadian Pacific Railway main line.

About twenty-three miles from Kamloops there is a lake known as Fish Lake, in which the fishing is so extraordinary as to border on the regions of romance, though locally it is considered a matter of course. For lake fishing, in point of numbers, it is impossible that this piece of water could be beaten; it is like a battue in shooting, the number to be caught is only limited by the skill and endurance of the angler; indeed, little skill is needed, for anyone can catch fish there, though a good fisherman will catch the most. Also fish can be caught on any day, some days being better than others, but a blank day is an impossibility. The lake is twenty-three miles south of Kamloops, and is reached by a good road, and there is now a small wooden house, where one can stop and hire boats. Ten years ago there was only a trail, which was rough travelling on horseback, with a pack horse to carry tent and provisions. The lake has been a fishing ground for the Indians from time immemorial, and fish used to be brought down by them to Kamloops from a fish trap built in the creek running out of the lake. I have also seen them fishing with bait and spearing fish at night; but the true bait for Fish Lake is the fly, and, contrary to the usual case, the white man with a fly and modern tackle can make catches which far surpass any that the Indian ever made. The trap has now been abandoned, and the Indians do not fish on this lake any more.

From time to time half-breeds and cowboys came into Kamloops with stories of big catches of trout made with a willow bough and a piece of string with a fly tied to it; sometimes 300 or 400 fish would be brought down which had been caught in this way.

This stimulated the sporting instinct of the inhabitants, and a few visits were paid to the lake and good catches were made, but the fishermen who went were of a very amateur kind. In the summer of 1897 an American proposed to me that we should go up and try what good tackle could do, in fact, he proposed that we should go up and try to make a record We went up in the first week of August, and the result far surpassed our wildest imagination. We fished three full days, and brought back 1500 trout, which weiged 700lb., cleaned and salted The first day we caught 350, for some time was wasted in finding the best places. The second day a start was made at 5 a m., and we fished till long after dark, about 9 30 p m , catching 650; the third day we caught about 500 The weather was intensely hot and fine, sometimes dead calm, sometimes a strong breeze, and at night a brilliant moon , but whether dead calm or blowing strong it made no difference to the fish, for they were taking as freely in the moonlight as at mid-day.

Flies were abundant, and the fish were ravenous for both real and artificial; they almost seemed to fight for our flies as soon as they touched the water. Even when almost every feather had been torn off they would take the bare hook. We fished with three flies, and often had three fish on at one time; on one occasion my companion handed me a cast and three flies with a few inches of running line which had been lost by me not twenty minutes before. The hottest and calmest hours of the day afforded the best sport, as is usual in my experience on all the waters of British Columbia, though wind did not make any difference, except to make it more difficult to manœuvre the boat. Our fish were cleaned and salted each day by some Indians, so that none were wasted, and no fish were returned to the water except the very smallest.

We had estimated our catch on the best day to be over 700 fish; but, owing to exhaustion and the necessity of cooking our supper, after being seventeen hours on the water, we did not feel equal to removing our fish from the boat, and during the night a raid was made on them by mink, which are very plentiful round this lake. Though it was impossible to say how many had been carried off, 650 was the exact total of fish counted on the following morning. If allowance is made for a rest for lunch, and time taken off for altering and repairing flies and tackle, it will be easily seen that this number of fish caught by two rods in one day on the fly constitutes a record which would be very hard to beat on this lake or any other. The best I was ever able to do again, with another rod, was a little over 300. But the conditions of the weather and the fly on the water were never quite so favourable. At the time mentioned this lake was little fished, and the Indians with their fish trap would catch in one day far more than we accounted for; but since the lake has become better known, and the fish trap has been abolished, it cannot be too much impressed on fishermen in this water that only the large fish should be retained. In 1903 we only kept eighty-four fish out of a total of 300 landed, and these weighed about 60lb.

This lake is a natural hatchery for trout, and its waters are alive with them; it is about four miles long, shaped like a boomerang; the margins are shallow, with a thick growth of rushes, among which the fish lie, feeding largely on a small brown fly, which may be seen on their stalks. In order to catch these, the fish may be seen jumping up and often shaking the fly into the water The best sport may often be had among these reeds in the more open places; but the fish must be held with a tight line, and prevented by main force from taking refuge among the roots of the rushes and entangling the cast among them. When this occurs a long willow wand with a salmon fly hook attached is an excellent means of landing a good fish, which could not be touched with a landing net.

The water of Fish Lake is very clear and always warm, suggesting the presence of some hot springs in the lake; though, if this is the case, it does not prevent its waters freezing in winter. The water in the centre of the lake is very deep, and fish may always be seen jumping there of a larger size than those usually caught. Few fish can be caught there by trolling a minnow or spoon, only an odd fish or so being the result; though a minnow or small spoon be trailed behind the boat for a couple of miles on the way home, nothing is caught. The fly is the only lure on Fish Lake. The average fish is from $\frac{1}{2}$lb. to $1\frac{1}{4}$lb., though fish of 2lb are common, while anything over 3lb. is unknown. I have seen several of 3lb , but nothing over it, and if larger fish lurk in the depths of the lake they have never been caught by Indian or white man. There is nothing but rainbow trout in the lake, and in general colour and appearance they vary very little, being handsome, bright-coloured specimens, very game and strong , the flesh is firm, and excellent eating when fresh caught. The altitude of this piece of water is between 4000ft. and 5000ft., which causes the nights to be cold and sometimes frosty even in August, while a cloudy day in these months is often chilly, causing a dearth of natural fly and some falling off in the sport. Should the wind be strong enough to prevent fishing on the big lake, there is a small lake at the western end which can be entered by a shallow channel, and often provides just as good fishing as the large one. Almost any ordinary Scotch loch flies are suitable for this water, a brown wing being perhaps the best, with a red body; the Zulu is a killing fly, as also a minute Jock Scott, size being the chief matter of importance. The fly must not be too large On our arriving one evening at the lake in most beautiful weather, two fishermen, who had just left the water after fishing hard all day, informed us that it was fished out, for they had only caught thirty fish of about 1lb. each; but the next day we caught 300, and the fishing was the same as ever, for the flies they had been using were Thompson ones, and the tail fly on one of their casts would have been too large on some Norway salmon rivers in low water.

It would be hard to conceive a more ideal place for fishing than this most beautiful lake, situated on a high plateau, surrounded by its reedy banks and flanked by woods of pine and birch, with waters of the deepest blue swarming with fish, while overhead is a cloudless sky. Ten years ago it was but seldom visited, now it is somewhat of a summer resort for the people of Kamloops, but it cannot be said to be overfished, as the season is very short—June, July, and August. Before and after that time the cold interferes with the rise of fly and the comfort of sportsmen. Formerly it was necessary to take a tent, and camp on the shores of the lake; but now an enterprising individual has put up a stopping house, which affords good enough accommodation for anyone visiting the lake, and also the use of boats. The last time I visited the lake, in 1903, the fishing seemed just as good as ever, and it will probably be some time before there is much falling off in this respect, unless the number of anglers who visit it is very much increased in the next few years. For though doubtless more fish are taken by the fly, yet the Indian fishing and the fish trap have been done away with. The latter would probably account for an immense number of fish, which are now saved to the lake; futhermore, there is no poaching of any kind, and the infamous otter is unknown in British Columbian waters. At the same time, the importance of returning small fish cannot be now too much impressed on all fishermen who try this water

Even in case Fish Lake should in time yield to the effects of overfishing, there are five other lakes known within a radius of a mile or two, which are believed to be just as full of fish, though, owing to the sufficiency of Fish Lake, their capabilities have been little tried, and it is chiefly on the reports of Indians that their reputation stands, though a few fish have been caught from the bank in one or two of them. It would be quite easy to put boats on them should the need arise, and larger fish are reported to abound in some of them Very probably the Indians are quietly fishing some of these lakes after deserting their old quarters In fact, all through this part of the country there are many lakes, some occasionally fished, and others almost unknown, and all abounding in trout A boat is necessary in all such lakes as have been alluded to; nothing can be done without one Mr Walter Langley uses a collapsible boat, which can be packed on a horse's back, and with this he has tried many lakes known to the Indians, his 22lb. trout was caught from this boat. In 1902 he visited some lakes on the opposite side of the

Thompson, about thirty-six miles from Savona's, and reported the most wonderful fishing to me. With a companion, he fished about five days, and brought back 700lb of salted trout; his catch included more than fifty fish of 4lb. in weight, and the average fish was about 2lb. There were no small fish in the lake they fished, and all were taken on the fly.

Mr Langley had accompanied me in 1900 to Fish Lake, where we had excellent fishing; but he reported the fishing on this lake to be far better, owing to the large size of the fish; in fact, he described it as the best fly fishing he had ever enjoyed. It may be noted that they had several Indians with them, and a large number of the fish caught were consumed on the spot, as a fish diet on such expeditions is a matter of necessity, in order to limit the number of pack horses required. It is fortunate that Indians are by no means averse to this article of food and seem very fond of fish of all kinds. Before the white man came to the country it must have been at many seasons of the year the staple article of food, and it is for this reason that the Indians know so well all the lakes and rivers where fish can be caught, making therefore good guides to a white man in search of new fishing grounds. But it must be remembered that the Indian does not use the fly, so that it is often necessary to make very careful inquiries from them as to the manner in which they catch fish in any fishing grounds that they may recommend; and such inquiries are very difficult to anyone not acquainted with their peculiarities and the Chinook jargon.

Many weird fish stories might be told about Fish Lake, but they become wearisome, and enough has been said to give some idea of the fishing to be obtained. It is, indeed, somewhat unique in its reality, and requires no Western embroidery of detail to be added to the facts quoted. These facts show, by the way, the immense fertility of the rainbow, where conditions are favourable, its fly-taking propensities, its boldness and voracity; all of which qualities will commend themselves to English fishermen, and confirm the enterprise and judgment of those who have introduced the fish into this country, where it seems to bid fair to equal, if not even to surpass, itself in the same good qualities

It is in the nature of a digression, perhaps, but as it has a bearing on the primitive methods of obtaining fish, the following account of a peculiar kind of fishing may be of interest here

There is a large lake in the interior, up the

Cariboo road, where the half-breeds indulge in a curious form of sport. A large portion of the lake is very shallow, and when it is frozen over the bottom can be very clearly seen. When this is the case some of the half-breeds go out on skates and mark trout through the ice, which they then pursue and attempt to drive into the shallowest parts near the shore. A fine fish is driven about until he appears to be quite exhausted, and finally is driven into shallow water, where he often hides under weeds at the bottom; a hole is then cautiously cut in the ice above him with a knife, through which he is speared A fish about 15lb. was once sent to me which had been caught in this way; it was not a trout, but the large kind of char, commonly known as Great Lake trout.

There is another lake called Mammit Lake, about twenty-five miles from Savona's and about fourteen from Fish Lake, which affords very good fishing. It is a large piece of water, about fifteen miles long, surrounded by open bunch grass hills, and can be reached from Savona's by a good road. Its name is derived from the large numbers of white fish called mammit which abound in its waters, and can only be taken by the net This lake is little fished, but several fishermen who have tried it are loud in its praises, notably my partner in the big catch on Fish Lake, who informed me that he had better sport on its waters, owing to the larger size of its fish, which appear to run about 2lb or so in weight, and few either smaller or larger. The evidence tends to show, however, that it is somewhat uncertain, possibly owing to its extreme liability to a good deal of wind, which may put down the fish or even prevent a boat from venturing on the lake. It would seem advisable for anyone who might wish to visit this water to arrange to camp there for a week or more, in order to be on the spot to sally forth whenever the fish are rising, for it would appear that this lake resembles Scotch lakes in the fact that the fish come on the rise at certain irregular times during the day, and in the intervals only a few can be caught by harling or trolling. I only once visited this water in August, but was entirely prevented from fishing owing to the high wind. The salmon had also entered the lake, and their presence is supposed to militate against good sport. July is the best time, and there is no doubt that very good fishing can be obtained there, while the lake is easily reached from Savona's, though there is no hotel accommodation, and it is necessary to take a tent and provisions for camping-out purposes.

Nicola Lake is about fifty miles from Kamloops, and can be reached by a bi-weekly stage. There is good fishing in the lake and in the river which flows into the Thompson at Spence's Bridge. The lake is a fine piece of water, over twenty miles long, and about a mile in breadth, nearly equal in size to Kamloops Lake. It has been but little fished, except by a few local anglers, and is full of very beautiful trout. I spent the summer of 1891 at the small hotel at the foot of this lake, but fished chiefly in the Nicola River, which flows out of it. The sport in the river gave me full occupation, so that very little time was devoted to the lake, for every day I caught as many fish as one could carry back to the hotel, mostly small, from $\frac{1}{2}$lb. to $\frac{3}{4}$lb., with one or two better fish of $1\frac{1}{2}$lb. to 2lb. At the place where the river left the lake I used almost to fill a boat with large chub and a few good trout; in the lake I made a few fair catches of a dozen or more fish about $1\frac{1}{2}$lb. But all the information I gathered then and since about this lake points to the fact that the best fishing is at the other end of it. In the river I used to catch a few fish very beautifully coloured about $\frac{3}{4}$lb., with red and black spots on a golden ground; in fact, I mistook them for brown trout, being ignorant of the fact that these fish were unknown in British Columbia. It is my belief that these were cut-throat trout. On a calm day fish can be seen moving all over the lake, which probably contains very large fish Mr. B Moore, now residing in Victoria, British Columbia, had a cattle ranch at its east end, and has often told me of the excellent sport he used to enjoy, both in the lake and the river which runs in there. Two hotels on the shores of the lake give good accommodation and keep a boat

In the autumn a little silver fish, about $\frac{1}{2}$lb. weight, runs up the streams from the lake in large numbers for spawning purposes, and is sometimes netted; it is very good eating, but takes no bait of any kind. The flesh is deep red. Locally it was supposed that these fish were a species of char, but in a pamphlet published by the Government of British Columbia on the fisheries it is stated: " There is another smaller form of the sockeye salmon, found in many of the interior waters, that appears to be a permanently small form, which is known to writers as 'the little red fish,' ' Kennerly's salmon,' or ' the Evermann form of the sockeye,' and which in some lakes of the province can be shown not to be anadromous. This form is often mistaken for a trout. It has no commercial value, and does not 'take a fly' or any bait. The Indians of Seton and Anderson lakes smoke them. They give them the name of 'oneesh.'" This is undoubtedly the fish which runs up the creeks from Nicola Lake in the early autumn to spawn in large numbers, at first bright silver like a salmon, turning to a crimson colour.

All are the same size; about $\frac{1}{2}$lb. They are sometimes sold in Kamloops for food. They are never seen in the lake, nor do I know if they return after spawning. This fish is also present in the Shuswap, but not in Kamloops Lake. The fishing in the Nicola River is very good as soon as it begins to clear and subside from the early summer floods, and it can be continued until the water gets too low in late August

These lakes and rivers above described are at present the best known in this district, but there are numbers of other lakes which are full of trout, some of which are fished by the Indians, and in time will doubtless become better known to fishermen. But it is quite evident that anyone visiting this part of the country has p enty of choice, and, in fact, would hardly find time to visit and thoroughly try all the rivers and lakes described This district of British Columbia has certain attractions of its own, not present in other parts; the climate is peculiarly fine and dry, with a most bracing and clear atmosphere. Except for an odd thunder shower, rain hardly ever falls, so that camp life is free from one of its chief drawbacks. Flies and mosquitoes are not so plentiful, though bad in certain places. The general aspect is much more open, with rolling hills of bunch grass and pine bluffs, which give the scenery a different appearance from other parts of the country.

CHAPTER VI.

The Kootenay district—Sawdust and Dynamite—Fine Sport in Vancouver—Harrison River and Lake—Big Fish in the Coquehalla—The Steel-head in the Fraser—Need for Better River Protection.

THERE are other parts of British Columbia which afford good fishing. Excellent sport is still to be obtained in the Kootenay district, which can be reached from Revelstoke on the main line of the Canadian Pacific Railway. Twelve years ago the fishing was unrivalled, especially on the Kootenay River. Very large bags could be got, though the fish were not quite as large as in the Thompson. But it is unfortunately true that since this district became a mining centre the fishing has been largely spoilt. Professional fishermen have fished for the market, sawmills have been allowed to empty their sawdust into the rivers, and probably alien miners and others have massacred wholesale with dynamite. In the coast district, of which Vancouver is the centre, there are plenty of rivers and lakes This part of the country has a heavy rainfall, which causes a thick forest growth to cover the country and render the streams difficult or even impossible to fish, unless they can be waded. This is a drawback from which the upper country rivers are free. But, still, fine sport can be had in many rivers and lakes. The Harrison River affords excellent fishing as early as April. The fish run from 1lb to 2lb., and take the fly freely. The river flows out of Harrison Lake to the Fraser at Harrison Station It must be fished from a boat Bags of thirty and forty fish are by no means uncommon. There is another river, whose name has escaped my memory, which is very good when low enough for wading, and flows into the Harrison Lake. The Hot Springs Hotel affords good accommodation.

If the Fraser is crossed at Hope Station there is a little village on the other side where somewhat rough accommodation used to be obtainable. The crossing was formerly done in an Indian log canoe, a means of transport which one would hardly recommend to anyone of a nervous temperament, though perhaps now a boat may be used A very beautiful river called the Coquehalla joins the Fraser at this place, which I used to fish in 1892 It consists of a series of fine pools and rapids for some distance, perhaps two or three miles, until an impassable canyon is reached, over which there is a natural bridge, and here, in the water below, immense trout may clearly be seen, though I know of no means of getting at them. At the time I fished this river, in July, the salmon were coming up, and I cannot say that my success was very great. I was, moreover, a stranger to the country, and could get no guide. Added to this, my tackle, experience, and skill were all of a very inferior order. But I found that the pools of this river contained very large fish, which were then to me quite unknown monsters, and I spent many long days on its banks in attempts to capture some.

I used to try each pool first with the minnow and then with the fly, which was, of course, exactly the opposite of the right course. Several good fish of 5lb. or so were landed and many lost. On one occasion, as I was hauling in a small trout to remove it from my fly, I was startled by an immense fish which leapt out of the water at it, close to my feet. It must have been a fish of anything from 10lb. to 15lb. or more. It jumped high in the air, drenching me with spray as it fell back into the water. I supposed it to be a large salmon, but as a bright red stripe was clearly seen along its side I know now that it was a rainbow trout. Twice in this river small trout were seized as they were being drawn in, but each time the single gut was snapped off by the fish. The higher parts of the river were never tried by me, though once or twice I saw large strings of trout brought in by cowboys. No doubt at this time of the year the best fishing was in the upper waters Probably the steel-head or sea-trout comes up the Fraser as far as the Coquehalla. Another stream called Silver Creek runs into the Fraser about three miles below Hope, and I had much the same experiences along its banks. It can only be fished when low enough for wading. I should much like to try these two streams again, as I am confident that some very large fish could be caught. It would be well worth trying the effect of a prawn, fished deep. A Silver Devon ought also to be effective. Personally this is the limit of my experience in British Columbia, but very good fishing is to be got in the Coquitlam and Capillano near Vancouver, and in the Stave and Pitt Rivers, which are a little further off. In all these rivers the steel-head can be got on the minnow, seldom, I believe, on the fly.

It is hard to say how far the steel-head may run up the Fraser—probably at least as far as the Coquehalla at Hope, for up to this point there is nothing in the strength of the current to prevent it; but above, in the Fraser Canyon, the tremendous difficulties of the ascent may well stop its further progress. The steel-head has not developed the powerful tail and anal fin of the Pacific salmon, which must be a great aid to it in passing through such strong water for such immense distances. It may well be that the smaller tail of the steel-head renders it unfit for the effort Otherwise, there would be no reason why it should not travel up the rivers as far as the salmon, just as the sea-trout does in European rivers. This is apparently not the case. The Fraser Canyon appears to be impassable to them, and they are only found in the lower tributaries of the Fraser and shorter coast rivers. The steel-head is the sea-going species of the rainbow; it is practically a silver rainbow, without the red stripe, which only appears faintly after it has been some time in fresh water. The steel-head is usually known as *Salmo gairdneri*, but in a recent letter Professor Jordan informs me that its correct name is *Salmo rivularis ayres*. He states that he has evidence to prove that the original *gairdneri* was the " nerka," which is the sockeye or blueback salmon

The smaller sizes take the fly readily under favourable circumstances, both in the salt water, at the mouths of rivers, and in the rivers themselves. The heavier fish of 7lb. and upwards are more often got on a minnow. Large ones up to 11 lb. have been caught with the prawn in the basin under the falls of the Capillano. Though I am not prepared to say whether these fish were rainbow or steelheads, the fact must be strongly insisted on that there is considerable difficulty in distinguishing between steel-head, rainbow, and the smaller salmon. In the case of the two former it is a matter of experience. The latter are easily known by the test of the anal fin and tail. Great confusion has been caused, and always will be, until proper care is taken.

The Coquitlam, Capillano, and other rivers have been much overfished by legal and probably by illegal means. The sport used to be excellent, and would soon improve again under proper conditions.

It would be an excellent thing if an anglers' club was formed in Vancouver, and part of the water preserved. If part of the water was thus properly treated, and a small hatchery put up, no doubt the fishing would soon be better than ever, while immense benefit would accrue to the remaining public water. This deplorable state of affairs is merely the natural result of the almost criminal neglect of the British Columbia Government to do anything to preserve the valuable sporting assets of the country. The Kootenay waters have suffered in the same way, as also some of the rivers near

Victoria on Vancouver Island. The Dolly Varden trout is very plentiful in all these rivers. Some very fine bags of large fish have been made in the Squamish River in Butte inlet. On Vancouver Island there is good fishing, easily reached from Victoria. The Cowichan River and Lake are the best known. Steel-head and rainbow can both be got on fly and minnow. The flies used are even larger than those on the Thompson. Personally, I have never fished on Vancouver Island, but from all that I have heard I should say that sport is not so good there as on the upper mainland.

CHAPTER VII.

*The Salmons of the Pacific—Legends Concerning Them—The Five Species—Systems of Migration—Powers of Endurance—Absence of Kelts—Do They Take a Fly?—Terrible Mortality—" A Vivid Red Ribbon "—Points of Difference Between the Quinnat and *Salmo salar*—Work of the Canneries—Artificial Propagation.*

NO account of the fishing in British Columbia would be complete unless some mention were made of the salmon, though it is only in tidal water that they can be caught with the rod, and though in the upper country they are useless from the fisherman's point of view. The annual migration of the Pacific coast salmon is a wonderful thing, about which little has been written, and much requires to be learnt. To those who have seen it, the phenomenon is most striking, and has vividly impressed the western imagination, which revels in weird stories concerning it. Thus it is current report that the waters of Harrison Lake have been known to rise several inches from some unknown cause, only to be accounted for by the immense rush of salmon into its waters; that paddle-steamers have been stopped in the Fraser and at sea by the salmon armies; that the backs of the fish have made stepping-stones by which the Fraser has been crossed.

These and similar stories are the folk-lore of British Columbia, and yet they are almost possible, so immense are the battalions of the salmon which swarm to the Fraser and other large rivers. It is an astonishing migration, full of interest and well worthy of study, not only to the naturalist, but to the student of social economy, as this migration is the source of an important food supply, and one of the chief industries of the country. There are fifty canneries established at the mouth of the Fraser, besides others further north, and between them they export annually millions of tins of canned salmon.

The Pacific coast salmon in British Columbia comprise five species, all belonging to the genus *Oncorhynchus* of the salmonidæ family. They are the king salmon or quinnat, a large fish running up to over 80lb., known also as the spring salmon; the silver and blue-back salmon, which are known as the cohoe and sockeye, and are the fish used by the canners; and the humpback and dog salmon, which are of little value, and only eaten by the Indians. The first named is the most interesting for the purpose of this book, as it is the fish which affords the famous sport at Campbell River. The silver and the blueback only run to about 10lb. The two last are pale fleshed, and are hardly considered fit to eat.

The king or tyee, quinnat, spring or chinook salmon (*O tschawytscha*) is the most important from the sportsman's point of view, but owing to its occasional white or very pale pink flesh not so useful to the canner. It runs from about 15lb to over 80lb.; fish of 50lb. are common, and some of 100lb have been reported It has sixteen rays in the anal fin. The back is blackish, and underneath it is not so bright a silver as the Atlantic salmon It turns black and not red in the upper waters

The sockeye or blue-back (*O. nerka*) is the chief source of the cannery supply. The anal fin is long, with fourteen rays. The back is blue and the sides of a bright silver changing to a dark green and dull crimson in the upper waters. Weight from 3lb. to 10lb. Flesh a deep red.

The cohoe, silver or fall salmon (*O. kisutch*) is also canned, weight 3lb. to 8lb, light green and silver in colour.

The dog salmon (*O. keta*), 10lb. to 12lb in weight, fourteen rays in anal fin. It is so called from the misshapen appearance of the head and teeth of the males at spawning time. Colour of a dark silver, turning black and reddish in the upper waters.

The humpback (*O. gorbuscha*), the smallest of the family, 3lb. to 6lb. A hump appears just behind the head of the males at spawning time, fifteen rays in the anal fin. The flesh of these last two species is not much used.

Of these fish the spring salmon appears first in the Fraser in the early spring, and progresses steadily up the river as far as it is possible to go, apparently keeping more up the main current and avoiding the Shuswap Lake to which the Thompson leads (at least it is very little noticed in that river), whereas the sockeyes swarm up it in great numbers It does not seem to travel in large schools in these waters. A few arrive in Kamloops Lake during July, but it is never much in evidence in the Thompson River district. It is doubtless a very powerful swimmer. Professor Jordan points out that this and the other species are remarkable for the great number of developed rays in the anal fin and tail, which must aid the fish immensely in its long journey against the strong water of the Fraser

The progress of all these fish is made by steady travelling in the slacker water at the sides of the river. I have often watched them slowly making their way upwards in the clear water of the Thompson, one noticeable fact being that they do not rise much to the surface or ever leap into the air, like our own fish. In the lakes, and occasionally in pools of the Thompson, I have seen them roll over in the water, but never leap into the air. It seems not unreasonable to suppose that one reason for the leaping of the Atlantic salmon is because he is practising for the time when he will have to jump a difficult waterfall in the river he ascends. But in the inland lakes and rivers the Pacific salmon never leap, and, in fact, are seen but little on the surface. On the other hand the trout appear to leap quite as much as the European species. On Fish Lake the rainbows are leaping continually.

The Pacific salmon has no skill in jumping, he merely swims on continuously; indeed, he appears perfectly incapable of negotiating the smallest waterfall. I have seen thousands of Pacific salmon stopped hopelessly by a fall which would not hinder a small European sea-trout. It may be that the tremendous nature of the journey already completed has robbed him of the energy necessary for leaping, but experience would lead me to believe that the Pacific salmon trusts to immense powers of endurance, which enable him to travel thousands of miles against a frightful current rather than to a short journey and one or two big jumps.

This fact is certainly worthy of further investigation and note, in view of the introduction into British Columbia of the Atlantic salmon. There must be numbers of rivers barred to the Pacific fish which would be quite easy of access to the Atlantic. I doubt much if the quinnat could tackle an ordinary artificial salmon ladder, though there are undoubtedly numbers of streams in British Columbia which could be rendered navigable to *Salmo salar* by such means. A small hatchery established on such a river might at once establish the European fish in these waters.

On the other hand it is very doubtful if the present attempt to acclimatise *Salmo salar* by the introduction of small fry into the Fraser can avail much. Few could hope to survive and compete with the countless myriads of the sockeyes, while it is doubtful if the Atlantic fish could ever make its way for hundreds of miles against the Fraser current. It is not fitted for a slow journey of weeks and even months, but rather for one of some few hours with a strong leap at the end which lands it at once in the destined pool or lake.

There are two other points which will strike the fishermen in British Columbia waters One is the absence of kelts at any time of the year. The other is the fact that, though the waters are often alive with young salmon, none are ever caught on the fly. The first point is explained by the fact that these fish die after spawning. There is no doubt that this is well established, though there is something to be accounted for—namely, the large specimens of each species, which must undoubtedly either be survivors of a former run or else fish which have stayed in salt water to a more advanced age To take the example of a spring salmon of 80lb.; this fish would, in Europe, be reckoned as at least ten years old and probably a great deal more Are we to conclude that such a fish has never been into fresh water before, or is it not more probable that he has only been in the habit of frequenting some lake at a short distance from the sea, and returning thence in time to escape death from exhaustion? The large specimens of the other species might also be accounted for in this manner.

The second point is merely a fact, and does not require any explanation, except that it may have some bearing on the matter of the adult fish not taking the fly. I would not go so far as to say that these young fish have never been known to take a fly, but I never remember catching one myself, and they certainly do not take it as the salmon parr do in our waters It is of course possible that many may be taken and supposed to be trout. But if such were the case, it would surely be more commonly known and noticed. Very little appears to be known of the habits of the young fish or the time they spend in fresh water before they go down to the sea.

It has been a much debated question as to whether the British Columbia salmon takes the fly, and it may be stated once for all that it does do so, but only in tidal waters. In the up-country lakes and rivers it takes nothing, and those who may have seen its migrations will easily understand the reason The fish have no time to feed or rest; they may be seen ceaselessly though slowly pressing on in the shallow water at the sides of the Fraser or Thompson, as if pressed on by the weight of those behind, impelled by some all-powerful desire to get to their journey's end, to spawn and die. None return, and the lakes and pools of the rivers are filled with corpses, on which bears, eagles, and all creatures which can eat fish are filled to the full.

There is no time to look at bait of any kind, for it is a terrible journey through the rapid waters of the Fraser, and many fish show the marks of bruises and cuts, while few are in an eatable condition by the time they reach Kamloops Lake.

This journey would seem to take them three or four weeks from the time they appear at the Fraser mouth, about 200 miles in distance. Anyone who has ever seen Hell's Gate, in the terrible canyon of the Fraser, and these millions of struggling fish slowly pushing their way upwards without a moment's rest, impelled by the *vis a tergo* of the swarms behind, and each one anxious only to move forward, can easily understand how impossible it would be in such a struggle for mere existence that a fish should pause to take bait. Even in our own rivers running salmon practically never take. It is only when they have reached some pool or resting-place that they will look at a lure. But when these masses of fish emerge into the large lakes, the first comers must still be remorselessly driven on by the mass of those behind until the farthest limits and some impassable barrier is reached. I have never seen the spawning-beds myself. Jordan says they spawn in 1ft to 3ft. of water in rivers like *salar*, but one can readily imagine the desperate struggle for existence that must go on as the swarms reach the grounds and fight for positions; while no doubt on their outskirts are small armies of trout and other fish eager to devour the eggs as soon as they are laid As the salmon seem to pass right up to the headquarters (*cf.* Jordan) they would get beyond the *big* trout. Probably it is here that their numbers protect them, the trout being unable to penetrate their close ranks until the eggs are laid and concealed in the gravel and death begins to be busy among the salmon. Possibly here, too, may be some protection, for doubtless the other fish prey on the dead carcases, which would be a more obvious food supply than the hidden eggs. This description of spawning-beds is mere imagination, as I have never met anyone who had seen them ; but it is probably much exceeded by the reality.

A short description of what I *have* seen will help to realise what must take place on the spawning-beds. It must be noted that the salmon runs are in cycles. Every fourth year is a big run of sockeye, and when there is a small run of these fish there may be a big run of humpbacks or dog salmon. One year in the early nineties the Thompson presented a strange sight to travellers in the Canadian Pacific trains, though as the trains pass this part in the very early morning probably few saw it. The line here closely follows the river, and in the canyon rises to several hundred feet above it, so that a splendid view of the river is obtained. At this time, as seen from above, the deep blue water of the stream was bordered on each side by a vivid red ribbon, which when seen closer proved to be the array of sockeyes struggling up the side eddies in countless myriads. How long this lasted I cannot say, but I saw it several times on my professional journeys on the railway. It was a very wonderful sight. Every fish was about the same size, about 7lb. or 8lb , and all were deep red in colour. The time of year was about September.

In 1901 I had occasion to go from Spence's Bridge to Nicola Lake in early September; the stage-route is along the banks of the river, which at that time was very low. A run of humpbacks was going on; the pools were black with them, and the shallows between the pools presented a most remarkable appearance; the water was only a few inches deep, and between the stones the humpbacks were slowly wriggling upwards in countless thousands, only half covered by the water. When the coach was high above the river they looked like an army of tadpoles blackening the river bed, their colour being almost black with a reddish tinge at the sides. The male fish alone has the curious hump well developed in the breeding season; it is situated just behind the head and is about ¾in. high, resembling the hump of a camel; the female has only a very small one. At an Indian village which we passed two or three Indians were standing in the water armed with long gaffs with which they hooked the fish out and threw them to the squaws on the bank, who were cleaning, splitting, and hanging them up on long fir poles to dry in the sun A rancher living near here informed me that he took the trouble to count the number on one pole and thereby estimate their total catch. I forget his figures, but believe it was several hundred thousand—a mere flea-bite to the total number of fish in the river, which must have run into millions. The fish were unable to get into Nicola Lake owing to a dam, and on my return journey, two weeks later, there was not a living fish to be seen, the pools being filled with dead bodies, and the awful stench of the river rising to heaven.

It seemed to me a terrible waste that all these fish should die, but such is the fact, and it must be fortunate that they do not feed on their way or they would clean out a river like an army of locusts. What becomes of the trout during these invasions presents a curious problem, for the condition of the stinking river would seem sufficient to kill them unless they can escape to some lake. Possibly the trout flee upwards ahead of the serried ranks of the invaders with the view also of feeding on their eggs when they reach the spawning grounds. I have seen the bottoms of good trout pools black with salmon in certain rivers and have been told it was useless to fish them, and this fact I also verified; while other pools higher up and not yet invaded gave good fishing

These two instances will give some idea of the extraordinary invasions by the salmon of the British Columbia rivers as it presents itself in the Thompson district

At the coast the migration begins with the large spring salmon, the quinnat, which seem to appear off the mouth of the Fraser in January, and run up the rivers during April, May, and June before the sockeyes make their appearance, but never in such large numbers as the latter. Their migration is more like that of the Atlantic fish, which they also resemble in point of size. They are not so much used by the canneries, whose season does not begin till July, and are only caught for the local market, and by trolling with rod and line; these are the fish which chiefly provide sport in the tidal waters of British Columbia.

As has been said they run up to 80lb and over, and resemble our own salmon in general appearance, though they are not of such a bright silver colour, and are rather more heavy looking. The most obvious point of distinction is the large size of the anal fin and tail, which contain a great many more rays than those of our own trout and salmon. This point of distinction is common to all the five species of the Pacific coast salmon, and distinguishes them from the rainbow and steel-head, which are true salmonidæ. The flesh, especially in spring, is excellent eating, but possibly not quite so delicate as the Atlantic fish, and not so highly esteemed. Perhaps this is partly owing to the fact that salmon is so common and cheap, for a large fish can often be bought for a shilling or half a crown.

I have seen an occasional large fish move in the Thompson early in July, but have never noticed them in the Kamloops Lake in any large numbers, though doubtless a certain proportion does come there. It would appear as if the large size and strength of this fish enables it to run earlier in the year and to stem the rivers when swollen by the melting snow in May and June; while the smaller sockeye times its appearance to coincide with the fall of the big rivers in July. It can hardly be a fact that the quinnat never returns to the sea, for if that were invariably the case, how could the large fish of 80lb., which must be of considerable age, be accounted for? It would not be difficult for a fish to return from a large lake like the Harrison, which is only some 50 miles or so from the Fraser mouth. It may be that if these fish get far up the Fraser, perhaps 500 miles or more from salt water, they may not have strength to return. Jordan says the spring fish run over 2000 miles in some rivers. But from spawning-grounds only distant a few miles they can easily return, as could also the smaller species, unless, which seems very unlikely, the act of procreation is fatal in itself. Still, the fact remains that I have never seen a kelt in British Columbia nor heard of one, nor does there seem to be any return stream of migration in winter or early spring, a feature which could not escape notice if it occurred to any considerable extent. Therefore if any fish return it must be only a few scattered individuals, not one in a million of the swarms seen passing upwards.

The Indians along the Fraser catch these fish by standing on certain rocks with a large dip-net, by which they catch a considerable number as the fish pass upwards

In the first week of July or thereabouts the silver and blue-back salmon appear, and the canneries at the Fraser mouth begin work This is the sockeye run, which is always very large, but varies in different years, every fourth year being an extra large one. Drift-nets are employed by a large number of boats, which may catch in one night thirty to eighty or more fish, for which they get about 15 cents. apiece from the canneries. The season lasts till about the end of August, when the run falls off, and is succeeded by the run of the humpback and dog salmon, which are of no commercial value. Indians, white men, and Japanese are employed, and the mouth of the Fraser is a scene of great activity, while on the American side large fish traps are employed in which many thousands of salmon are caught at one haul. The following will give some idea of the work of the canneries. :—

ANNUAL PACK FOR SIX YEARS

1897	1,027,204 cases (48lb).
1898	492,657 ,, ,,
1899	765,517 ,, ,,
1900	606,530 ,, ,,
1901	1,236,156 ,, ,,
1902	625,982 ,, ,,

The first news of the approach of the sockeye is generally brought to Vancouver or some other coast city by some sailing ship or steamer which has encountered them in the straits of San Juan or the Gulf of Georgia. Often strange stories are told of moving through a vast salmon army, perhaps seven miles broad and of unknown length, all heading straight for the Fraser's mouth, from their unknown feeding-grounds in the North Pacific. Wild as some of these tales seem, yet they are more or less true. For these immense shoals come through the San Juan Straits and head northwards up the British Columbian coast towards Alaska, while only a mere detachment enters the Fraser, a detachment of a few millions. And also if it be true that none return, they can have no leaders to show the way, but must retrace the route they took as smolts on their way from the river to the ocean, impelled by the sexual instinct to propagate the species. They appear to hang about the mouth of the Fraser for a short time, then advance upwards as far as it is possible to go, hundreds of miles into the interior, and up every stream which will permit of their progress, where they eventually spawn and die.

The silver salmon and blue-backs run in separate shoals, and their respective names show the difference between them. Very handsome fish are they in spring, of a bright silver hue resembling a fresh run grilse, and about seven or eight pounds in weight. But they quickly become red, and in the upper waters of the rivers often present a far from healthy appearance, showing visible traces of their struggles with the rocks and whirlpools encountered in their ascent This well-known red appearance is not, however, altogether due to the effects of the fresh water, for straggling late bands are described as entering through the Straits of San Juan in the autumn which are almost as red as their earlier fellows at that time in the upper waters of the Fraser.

On the heels of the sockeye come the humpback and the dog salmon, about the same in size, and fine silvery fish before the breeding season sets in. But it is late in the autumn when they arrive, and their flesh is white and does not meet the demands of the market. The so-called hump is only present in the breeding season.

An attempt was made to can and sell them as white salmon, but without success ; though recently a market has been found in Japan, whither they are sent in the dried form. Japan, by the way, possesses a sixth species of *Oncorhynchus*, the masu, a fish resembling the humpback, but this is not known to British Columbian waters.

Although an immense toll is taken by the canneries, yet the supply of fish still continues, assisted by the hatcheries which have been supplied by the Government of Canada, by whose aid it is hoped that the effects of over-fishing will be counteracted. For this hope there is considerable ground, as the fishing on the Columbia River has been restored by this means to something of its former condition.

CHAPTER VIII.

The Diplomat and the Salmon—The Struggle for Existence—Salmon and Steel-head Liable to be Confused—Sport in Tidal Waters—The Campbell River—The Pioneers—A River of Fifty-Pounders—Smaller Salmon on the Fly—Method of Fishing—Tackle—Typical Good Bags—The Steel-head—Cost of Fishing—Dangers of Over-Fishing for Canneries—A Good Trolling Time.

THOUGH much more might be written about the canning industry and the migration of the salmon, it is not material to the purpose of this book, and has only been touched on to show how it bears on the question of salmon fishing by rod and line; for it is often stated that the salmon does not take the fly in British Columbia, as if it were a personal matter and some perverse characteristic of the fish. There is another story very popular in the west, relating what happened at the time when the great fur companies held the country and were disputing and even fighting for its possession. The Imperial Government sent out some illustrious diplomat to report on the situation, and he described the country as of no value and so hopeless that " even the salmon would not take the fly." It is a tradition in British Columbia that on this ground the now flourishing States of Idaho, Montana, Washington, and Oregon were handed over to the Americans. The description given of the conditions under which the salmon migrate is intended to show reasons why the fish are unable to oblige the angler in this matter of taking the fly. These conditions are obvious. The desperate struggle for existence in an immense shoal of fish pressing upwards against the tremendous current of a river abounding in strong rapids and whirlpools; the length of the journey, several hundred miles in extent; the absence of any chance of resting owing to the pressure of the multitudes behind; and, finally, the state of exhaustion brought on by all these forces combined—these things must, and indeed do, reduce the fish to such a condition that its final energies are devoted to and exhausted by the propagation of its species. Even if enough vitality were left to make it take a bait, no sport would be obtained by the angler, and his sorry capture would be generally unfit for food.

I have once or twice experimented by foul-hooking salmon in the tail in the Nicola River, but after one feeble rush the fish was easily hauled ashore even by light trout tackle, and returned to the water as entirely useless to anyone except an Indian.

There is only one final conclusion to be drawn, that in the upper waters of the rivers and the inland lakes the salmon do not take the fly or any other bait, nor is there any case in which it has been even alleged that a salmon has ever been caught on the fly. Occasionally large silvery fish have been caught on spoon and minnow, but, in the absence of proof to the contrary, it is most probable that these fish are either large silver trout, rainbow, or steel-heads. Absolute proof of the capture of a salmon is still wanting, though it is quite possible that such a thing has occasionally taken place.

The question of salmon taking the fly in the tidal waters is another matter, for there is not the least doubt that all the five different species have been taken in this manner; though possibly not so often as is stated, because the steel-head is a source of error, from its resemblance to the salmon A fish of 15lb. is taken on the fly and the capture of a salmon is announced, on the strength of its weight and size; whereas, on inquiry, it is found that the fisherman is certain that it was a salmon, but can produce no evidence to prove that it was not a steel-head. It is not everyone who can tell the difference between a salmon and a steel-head on its mere appearance without counting the rays on the anal fin or tail, and until this simple proof is put to the test there will always be a doubt as to the frequency with which the salmon is taken on the fly

The size of the anal fin is so obvious a distinction of the Pacific salmon that I have often observed it in numbers of small fry caught for bait, the fin in a small fish two or three inches long resembles the wavy fan-like fins seen in the Japanese gold fish, and distinguishes it at a glance from the corresponding short fin of the young rainbow. A curious error of this kind occurs in Mr. Rudyard Kipling's well-known book, "From Sea to Sea," where he describes most enthusiastically a day's salmon fishing in California on the Sacramento, and his capture of numerous salmon on the fly There is no doubt that his fish were steel-heads.

There is enough evidence from various sources to show that the salmon take the fly in tidal waters, but it cannot be said that there is much to show that they do so very freely, especially in the case of the large quinnat salmon But, on the other hand, the spoon bait is taken most greedily by all the different species. It may be that the fly has not been tried as much as it might have been owing to the success of the spoon. The result is that at present trolling in these waters with this bait is the chief means employed, and has afforded sport unrivalled of its kind by any other part of the world.

Very fair sport can be got in the Narrows near Vancouver or in the sea off Esquimalt or Oak Bay near Victoria. But the place which has of late years been distinguished by the most extraordinary salmon fishing ever heard of is the mouth of the Campbell River on the east coast of Vancouver Island. In the places first named, as also at the mouths of several well-known rivers, salmon and steel-heads may be caught by trolling and spinning, and occasionally with the fly. Thus seven or eight fish are no unusual bag in the waters near Victoria, but they are not usually of any very great size. The mouth of Campbell River appears to be the only place yet known where the big salmon can be caught in any large number, though it is quite possible that other places exist.

This river has long been a fishing ground for the Indians, who trolled for the fish with a strong hand-line and spoon. The pioneers of this fishing among white men were Mr. G. P. FitzGerald and Sir Richard Musgrave, who made an expedition to these waters in the early nineties and camped at the mouth of Campbell River, also trying Salmon River and other places along the coast. They met with great success in the tidal waters off Campbell River, but practically drew a blank wherever else they tried. It was on this occasion that Sir R. Musgrave landed a 70lb. salmon, which holds the record in these waters. Since then an increasing number of fishermen have visited Campbell River, until of late years there have always been a few rods on the ground; and a small hotel has been put up. There is, however, not much fear of over-fishing, though the time is past when a fisherman could have the whole of the water to himself.

There are sinister rumours of a cannery and fish traps to be established in the near future, and should these things come to pass then the fishing which has been enjoyed will become a mere memory and perhaps these pages its only record.

Mr. FitzGerald always enjoyed his best sport under the guidance of an Indian, and by employing the Indians' spoon, which is a plain silver spoon with a loose hook. The main aim was always the large 50lb. fish, smaller fish of 25lb. or so being regarded as a nuisance, and if possible shaken off the hook. The biggest catch was eight fish six of which were about 50lb apiece; anyone familiar with salmon fishing will know that this is no small feat after allowing for fish hooked and lost, while it must be remembered that a fish of 50lb. may take over an hour to land. Sir Richard Musgrave's large fish of 70lb. took an hour and a half to land; it was a magnificent fish, the record salmon of the rod and line. A cast of it was shown at Farlow's, in the Strand, and also at Rowland Ward's, in Piccadilly, during the spring of 1897. The spoon fishing of the Namsen and other Norwegian rivers fades into insignificance beside such sport; two or more fish of over 50lb. were the average catch, besides more that were hooked and lost, while the numerous smaller fish were not considered worthy of notice.

Mr. A. Duncan reports excellent success with the prawn, which he was the first to use, and it may be that with this deadly bait even larger fish might be obtained. · He also reports that with a silver-bodied fly in the evening, but at no other time, he caught large numbers of salmon about 7lb. in weight, and could have filled a boat with them. He gives no absolute proof as to whether these fish were salmon or steel-heads, but it is his opinion that they were salmon

The fishing is done by crossing and re-crossing the small bay into which Campbell River flows, trolling from a canoe or small boat, the breadth of the water being about half a mile; the method is exactly like trolling in a Norwegian fiord just off the mouth of a river. It is a curious fact that no sport can be obtained in the river itself, which fully supports the contention put forth above that the Pacific coast salmon ceases to take as soon as it begins to run, the taking fish being those which are hanging about the mouth of the river preparatory to running up. There seems to be no instance of the very large fish taking the fly.

There is no need to say much as to tackle, except that it should be strong and that there should be plenty of line. The native spoon can be obtained on the spot. Some fishermen prefer a large rod as better able to hold off a fish which runs under the boat; I should personally prefer a short, stiff, steel-centred rod such as Hardy's 12ft. Murdoch—a type of rod preferred by the Americans for yellow tail and tuna fishing. This kind of rod is much handier in a boat, and almost unbreakable.

The following is a list showing some of the bags at Campbell River.

Mr. A. Duncan in 1904. Tyee salmon, eighteen; weight, 810lb. Average, 45lb. Cohoes and tyee under 30lb, thirty-two Total, fifty fish in eighteen days. Best day August 9th, 1904. Seven salmon,

Fishing in Campbell River.

56lb., 53lb., 52lb., 16lb., 12lb., 7½lb., and 4lb. The eight heaviest fish: 50¾lb., 56lb., 53lb., 52lb., 52lb., 50lb., 48½lb., and 48lb.

Mr Duncan says:

Fish under 30lb. are counted as grilse. The cohoe salmon will take a fly; white with silver tinsel, I found best. They take in the sea at sunrise and sunset when they are jumping—in fact, more could be got in this way while they are actually jumping than by trolling, only they must be jumping and also fairly plentiful. I have got an odd one casting, but nearly all by trailing the fly. They give splendid sport on a light trout rod The largest I got last year (1903) was 12lb. But they were not "running" this year, and I only got two of 7lb. each on the fly. Salmon are caught in Cowichan Lake (after ascending 30 miles of river); frequently I got one myself and saw others caught, though they are black and ugly. But I am told on absolutely reliable authority that great sport is had with tyee salmon (from 30lb. downwards) on the fly in the Cowichan River in the spring, and then only when the water is discoloured. They only take the fly sunk, and generally a leaded one is used.

It is noteworthy that this peculiarity of only taking the fly when jumping is also common to the trout in the Shuswap and other large lakes in the interior. Also their favourable time is at sunrise and sunset. It might also be noted that Mr. Duncan makes no mention of the steel-head or sea-trout. This fish runs in the Cowichan River and Lake in the spring. The test of the number of rays in the anal fin and tail should be applied to all these fish.

The sockeye does not appear to frequent Campbell River. The tyee and cohoe frequent the coastal waters of British Columbia. But the feeding ground of the sockeyes is some unknown part of the Pacific Ocean from which they migrate and enter the waters between the mainland of British Columbia and Vancouver Island in great shoals, through the Straits of San Juan. Even then their stomachs are empty and contracted, showing that they have already travelled some distance Mr. Babcock, the Fisheries Commissioner of British Columbia, states in his report for 1903. "The first fish are reported from Otter Point. From Sherringham Point east their movement is clearly defined as they pass close in shore They come in rapidly with the flood tides, at times close to the surface and breakwater; frequently during the last weeks of July and the first two weeks in August, in years of large runs, they show themselves plainly, a racing, leaping, bluish silver mass in the clear and rapid moving waters." Then they appear to strike the discoloured water of the Fraser, and follow it to the mouth of the river. In 1903, 2,948,333 sockeyes were delivered to the canners during the last two weeks of July and the month of August.

The steel-head trout (*Salmo gairdneri*) is the

anadromous form of the rainbow, bearing the same relation to it as our sea-trout does to the brown trout. It more closely resembles in form, colour of flesh, and habit the Atlantic salmon than any other form found on the Pacific coast. It spawns in fresh waters, and survives after spawning and returns to the sea. It feeds in fresh and salt water. How far it penetrates into the interior and up the Fraser is a matter of doubt. My own opinion is that it only goes as far as Hope, being unable to face the strong water in the Fraser Canyon, owing probably to the fact that it is not equipped with the powerful anal fin and tail of the Pacific salmon. It enters all waters near the coast, and is caught on the rod in the Stave and Pitt Rivers I have never heard of one being caught on the Thompson. Trout fishermen in the coast rivers catch them with both fly and minnow.

The following details of catches are quoted from an article which appeared in *The Field* in December, 1905, from the pen of Mr. L. Layard. In 1904 twenty-four tyee weighing 1,004lb., average 41$\frac{1}{2}$lb.; forty-three cohoes weighing 297lb, average 7$\frac{1}{2}$lb. Best fish 49lb., 49lb, 50lb, 51lb., 53lb, 53lb., 55lb., and 56lb. He also states that he saw two fish of 60lb, landed. In 1905, for July and August, fishing for thirty-eight days.

six hundred and eighty-eight salmon weighing 5,254lb. Best fish, 50lb. Best catches, thirty-six fish (275lb.) in five hours, forty-four fish (330lb.) in six hours

A Mr J. Pidcock, fishing for his cannery from 3 a.m to 9 p.m, in a dug-out, using two hand lines, caught 706 salmon. Mr Layard speaks very well of the new hotel, and of a Mr. J. Thompson as boatman. He quotes the hotel charges as £2 a week and 2s. a day for a fine sea boat, and 12s. a day as wages for a boatman.

He gives some interesting particulars of Campbell River itself, to which a trail is to be cut from the hotel. There seems to be good rainbow trout fishing for two miles in the river. The salmon are stopped by a waterfall, where there is a large pool 30 feet deep, in which tyee salmon, with humpback, cohoes, and trout, could be clearly seen Mr. Layard could not induce them to touch anything from the bank, but a tyee of 18lb was hooked on a spoon and lost two days afterwards by another man from a canoe. The Indians stated that such a thing as hooking a salmon in the river had never been heard of in their traditions. No mention is made of the steel-head, and there is no proof given that the above was not one of these fish. Mr. Layard was not equipped for fly-fishing, but believes that the cohoes would have taken the fly.

An examination of these catches shows beyond dispute that there has never been such salmon fishing as this in any other waters, and fortunate indeed were those who first enjoyed it. Even yet the sport is there, as Mr. Layard shows, and perhaps may still go on for many years yet. In spite of adverse prophecies, possibly the cannery and fish traps may never be built, for the quinnat is mostly useful to the angler Unfortunately nothing can be done to save this splendid piece of fishing unless all the land and foreshore rights were bought up by some philanthropist in the interests of sport, which is hardly within the bounds of possibility, whereas if an offer for these rights is made to the Government, for the purposes of fish-trap and cannery, a refusal is impossible. Let us hope and even pray that no cannery is ever built, and even if it is that it may soon be abandoned, for though I am myself a fly-fisherman and think that trolling is only a poor imitation of the real thing, yet in this place the great size and number of the fish make up for other deficiencies, fulfilling the desires of the most ardent salmon fisherman, and surely satisfying his wildest dreams.

The fishing at Campbell River can be enjoyed

from June to September, and steamers call there about twice a month on their way from Victoria to the north; formerly it was necessary to take a tent and provisions and camp out, but now accommodation can be got at the hotel. July and August are the best months.

The best rod for Campbell River, as I have said, would be an 11ft. or 12ft rod of the pattern of Hardy's Murdoch, a steel-centred split cane; the reel should carry at least 80yds. of line and 100yds. of strong backing; it would be well to carry a spare line. Traces and casts should be taken, but spoons could be got better on the spot or in Victoria. Tackle for fly-fishing might well be taken also.

The Americans use at Catalina for tuna fishing a line called cuttyhunk line; it is very thin, light, and of tremendous strength. It is called "twenty-four strand" line, the strongest man could not break it with his hands, and yet it is not as thick as a salmon casting line. It makes splendid backing for a casting line, and as a trolling line it is absolutely unequalled. The size which will make good backing for a trout line is nine strand, and is very hard to break with the hands Twenty-four strand is unbreakable; it only succumbs to the mighty tuna when the whole line is run out

Another advantage is that it is absurdly cheap, a 1,000 yard tuna line only costing £1. Three or four hundred yards would go on an ordinary salmon reel and would form a splendid trolling line. If I remember rightly, they use twelve strand line for yellow tail fishing at Catalina, and consider it quite strong enough. The yellow tail is a mackerel running from 25lb. to 60lb , and is believed to be stronger and fiercer for its size than the tuna. The cuttyhunk line is, however, absolutely useless for anything except trolling ; it is far too light for casting a fly or even for throwing a minnow or any other kind of bait It must also be well waxed with a piece of ordinary yellow beeswax to prevent it rotting, because it has no kind of dressing or protection from the effects of water. It would need waxing at least twice a week. I have never seen this line except in California, though it can probably be obtained anywhere in the United States. In my opinion it is far superior in strength to any of our English lines for trolling, while the price of a sufficient length for ordinary purposes would be about half a crown.

It is more than probable that other rivers will become known before long where the fishing may rival that of Campbell River. The sea coast of British Columbia stretches far to the north, and most of it is absolutely unknown to the fisherman, while even further north-still there are canneries on the coast of Alaska I have seen salmon in Dawson City which looked quite fresh run and had been netted in the Yukon; also grayling which had been caught on the fly in the Klondike River. If ever the present known rivers of British Columbia are fished out, there is surely an inexhaustible supply further north. There can be no question but that the Grand Trunk Pacific will in a few years open up a new country of lakes and rivers, in which the sport should be at least as good as those already known.

The fishing at Campbell River is apparently not confined to the mouth of the river—at least in good seasons—as Mr Layard speaks of fishing up and down both sides of the strait from Seymour Narrows to Cape Mudge lighthouse, a distance of 12 miles. A grant from the Government has been made for a pier to be built at Campbell River, enabling all steamers to call there, which will render it more easy of access

CHAPTER IX.

Recapitulation of Salmon and Trout Problems—Importance of Preserving British Columbian Fisheries—Possibility of Introducing Atlantic Salmon—Question of Altering Present Close Season for Trout—Past and Present Neglect of Trout Fisheries—Need for Governmental Action—Difficulties in the Way of It—Conclusion

IT will be very evident to those who have read the foregoing chapters that there is a great deal to be learnt about the fish that inhabit the British Columbian waters, and that several interesting problems require solving. These facts should render the greater interest to the fishing. The salmon perhaps present the most difficult questions, for their life-history is evidently almost unknown Their eggs germinate in the hatcheries, and the fry are turned out into the lakes, but from that moment to the time they return from the sea their movements are unknown. It is not known at what age they seek the salt water, nor at what age they return; while in the case of the sockeye their feeding grounds in the Pacific are an unsolved mystery

The most interesting trout problem is the identity of the silver trout of the Kamloops and the

Okanagan Lakes, whether it is a distinct and new species, or merely a variety of the rainbow.

The identity and life-history of the small silvery fish which runs from the Nicola, Anderson, and other large lakes into the small streams ought to be a matter of some interest. This fish has been alluded to as a miniature sockeye It certainly presents the curious phenomenon of a sockeye run in miniature from the deep waters of the lake into the small streams, where it also turns red and spawns. It does not seem to be known whether it also dies after spawning. It certainly takes no bait of any kind.

In concluding this most imperfect attempt to give some slight idea of the fishing in these waters, it is certainly not out of place to allude to the immense importance and necessity of preserving the fishing for the future. It is but lately that the British Columbian Government seems to have awakened to the great importance of its fisheries, and even yet it seems but little to appreciate the actual value and even more perhaps the potential value of its inland waters from a sporting point of view. It is almost superfluous to point out, in illustration, the value of the sporting rights of the rivers of Norway and Scotland and their large annual rental.

The value of the British Columbian rivers in this respect is at present only small, serving merely as an attraction to a few visiting anglers from England and the States, and a fishing ground for the residents of the country. But even so they form one of the chief attractions of the country, and will undoubtedly become more important, while their potential value if the Atlantic salmon could be introduced is hard to estimate. The evidence brought forward tends to show that the Pacific fish is fitted for long journeys entailing more endurance and greater swimming powers than the Atlantic fish possesses, but that the latter can leap small waterfalls which are impassable barriers to the former. One fish is a long distance runner, the other is a hurdle racer.

This fact is fully worthy of further investigation and thought. It might lead to important results. By introducing small hatcheries which would only cost a few pounds on suitable streams, the Atlantic fish might be introduced in a few years. Salmon ladders might be placed round falls which this fish could easily surmount, though they would be impossible to the Pacific species, and by this means numerous useless streams could be turned into valuable salmon rivers. From the lease or sale of such rivers the Government would reap a handsome reward. The Atlantic fish would probably have no difficulty in holding its own in the sea, for the shoals of herring and oolachan would afford an ample food supply

Large silvery fish have been caught, as has been said in a former chapter, in a certain part of the Shuswap Lake by surface trolling, whose exact identity is not well established, though they are probably silver trout. Also many silvery fish have been caught lately on the minnow at the mouth of the Nicola River where it joins the Thompson at Spence's Bridge. These fish have been alleged to be salmon, though no proof has been given that they are such They have always been caught late in the autumn, at which time all salmon would be red and out of condition. These fish might be steel-heads, but it is far more probable that they are silver trout, collecting at the mouth of the Nicola preparatory to running up it for spawning purposes

It is quite certain that very large rainbow and silver trout inhabit the deep pools of the Thompson, but as yet no one appears to have captured any of very large size on the rod. Possibly if the pools were tried later in the fall, when the river has become low, by deep fishing with live or dead bait, or the prawn, some very large fish might be landed. The best time to attempt this fishing would be after the present close season on October 16th or very early in the spring as soon as the ice has gone. It is thought by the local anglers that the present close season might well be extended for another month or so, to the middle of November. For in October the rainbow are in splendid condition and show no signs of spawning Conversely, the spring season might be delayed, as many stale fish can be seen in May and even in July. It is quite certain that the rainbow spawns very late in the year, and further inquiry into this question is needed.

It is unfortunate that trout have had little but nominal protection in British Columbia. Their best protection has hitherto been natural conditions and the social condition of the country—many fish and few fishermen. For in a new and sparsely settled country there is no wealthy leisured class who have much time to devote to fishing. Also many rivers and lakes have been difficult of access. But these conditions cannot last; they have changed much in the last ten years and are now changing still more, in some districts not without more or less disastrous results. Vancouver City has now grown to be a large place with some forty thousand people, and the fine fishing of the

Coquitlam and Capilano is almost a thing of the past. The Kootenay mining district has been opened by railways, and the once phenomenal fishing at Slocan Falls and round Nelson has immensely fallen off; report says that here it has been ruined by market fishing or worse, and in other parts of the province saw mills have been allowed to dispose of their waste in the rivers, and dynamite has been used for other purposes than mining. And though the white man is liable to be occasionally pulled up by the law, the Indian is apparently allowed to use spear, net, and salmon roe without any interference.

The same remarks apply generally in the same way to the protection of large or small game. The Nemesis which has fallen on many of the States of the Union will undoubtedly overtake British Columbia unless the Government fully rouses itself to the urgency of the matter before it is too late and before these invaluable assets of the province have passed away for ever. Many States of the Union have enacted too late the most stringent game laws, and have spent vast sums in vain attempts to restore what British Columbia still possesses and which could be so easily retained at but a trivial expense and by the exercise of a little foresight and trouble

For some years small societies for the protection of game and fish have existed in Vancouver, Victoria, and Kamloops, and, with most praiseworthy perseverance in a good cause, have attempted to rouse public opinion and stimulate the Government to take action. And it would appear that at last their pertinacity has met with some measure of reward, for the Government has appointed a head game-warden for the whole province and local wardens for different districts. This method of game preservation has been employed for many years in the older parts of Canada and is in vogue in California, Montana, and probably all the States If properly carried out it should be of great benefit to British Columbia.

In the past, unfortunately, whenever the question of game protection was brought up in the Provincial Parliament, the ridiculous cry of " class legislation " was always heard, generally raised by some labour member. It should be quite clear to anyone that an efficient game law and efficient provision for carrying it out will preserve sport for everyone equally. The poor man is just as fond of fishing as the rich, when he can get it; and the sacred fire burns as brightly in both peer and peasant. But the rich man can buy a river or a tract of land and preserve it for himself; and this he can do just as easily, and far more cheaply, in British Columbia than in Norway and Scotland. Therefore the best way is to preserve the game and the fish, so that there may be sport for all, rich and poor alike. As they say in California, " preserve it for the people and by the people." For unless this is done and proved effectual, the time will soon come when the wealthier people will form clubs for both shooting and fishing, and private game preservation will close gradually the free waters of the province.

There have been other obstacles to proper protection. A most mischievous and, I am firmly convinced, most false argument on the part of the salmon canners has often been alleged as a strong reason why no protection should be given to trout and why the law of the province should be disregarded. The canners state that the trout are the salmon's worst enemies, destroying both eggs and young. There is, of course, no question as to the truth of this accusation. But the reasoning deduced from it is wrong. It is quite impossible to destroy all the trout in the British Columbia waters; and if it were not, no possible advantage would be gained by so doing, because, by the inexorable laws of the survival of the fittest and of supply and demand, the position of the trout would be occupied by other fish which prey on the eggs and young of the salmon. The decrease of trout would be supplied by an increase in the numbers of the squaw fish and various species of char which are just as bad enemies of the salmon.

Both the Federal and Provincial Governments are afraid to prevent the Indians from taking fish or game in or out of season or to interfere in any way with their usual methods of procuring them for food. The Federal Government is the worst offender, because it erroneously believes that if the Indians were in any way curtailed in their food supply, the Government might have to supplement the want by rations, and thus be put to great trouble and expense. It is as well to note that the Indians are under control of the Federal Government On the other hand the Indians are amenable to the laws of the Province, except under certain conditions on their own reserves, which in British Columbia are very small, generally merely a few acres. The Provincial Government is, however, naturally unwilling to act in opposition to the wishes of the Federal power.

This attitude of the Federal Government is based on ignorance of the actual conditions in British Columbia. The Indians of the province are self-supporting and very good workers, having long ceased to depend on hunting and fishing for their livelihood. They differ most essentially from the Blackfeet and Crees of the plains. The British Columbian Indian is quite capable of understanding the fact that it is inadvisable to kill game or fish during the breeding season. Except, perhaps, in the most remote parts of the province, he should be promptly taught that he is just as much liable to penalties under the Game Act as the white man. It would take a very short time to enforce the lesson, and until it is done no Game Act will ever be really efficient, because the white man will never respect and keep a law which is not enforced on Indian and white alike.

This small volume is merely intended to give some idea of the fishing in British Columbian waters, from facts gathered in twelve years' experience of the province. It probably contains errors of commission, perhaps, as well as of omission, and makes no claim to be authoritative in scientific detail. But at least it contains some of that strange fish lore which can be only gained on the river bank and by intercourse with others of the same craft It fairly represents what is at present known among the fishermen of the province, with almost all of whom I am personally acquainted. It is my sincere hope that someone better qualified will, in the near future, deal more ably with the subject.

The ordinary Englishman often appears to be under a strange delusion that British Columbia is situated in a part of the world which he vaguely alludes to as South America, and it is somewhat curious that the country is not better known, for it is a glorious land of great mountains, forests, streams, and rolling hill, in which game and fish are very plentiful, with a climate and conditions of life peculiarly suited to Englishmen, especially those who have the instinct of sport. An attempt has here been made to describe the fishing; but there is also fine big game shooting, for the interior fastnesses of Vancouver Island are the home of thousands of that finest of the deer tribe, the wapiti; in the northern forests and the mountains moose, sheep, goat, and bear are numerous; everywhere the large mule deer is common; ducks and geese abound in the waters.

The soil of the valley is very fertile; gold, silver, copper, lead, iron, and coal are among the natural products; there is an inexhaustible supply of the finest timber in the world

Surely British Columbia is a splendid jewel—still rough-hewn and uncut, it may be, but one which will yet shine forth as one of the brightest stars in the Imperial diadem.

CHAPTER X.

TUNA FISHING AT AVALON, SANTA CATALINA ISLAND.

> I go
> To the island-valley of Avilion;
> Where falls not hail, or rain, or any snow,
> Nor ever wind blows loudly; but it lies
> Deep meadow'd, happy, fair with orchard-lawns
> And bowery hollows crown'd with summer sea.
> *The Passing of Arthur.*

THE lines placed at the head of this chapter are in many ways not inappropriate to Santa Catalina Island, with its little village of Avalon, though meadows and lawns are somewhat conspicuous by their absence.

For there can be little doubt that the name is connected with the Arthurian legend, and must have been brought to this far-off land by the early Spanish monks 200 years ago. No doubt the peaceful silence of the island and the deep blue of the summer sea reminded one of them of some island in distant Spain, where the great king is still sleeping. To quote " Fiona McLeod ":—

This tradition is found among every European people. Where is Joyeuse Gard? Some say it is in the isle of Avillion off the Breton shores ; some say it is in Avalon, under the sacred hill of Glastonbury.

Arthur himself has a sleeping place (for nowhere is he dead, but sleeps, awaiting a trumpet call) in "a lost land," in Provence, in Spain, under the waters of the Rhine.

The Californians have fortunately retained many of their beautiful Spanish names, instead of changing them into Anglo-Saxon vulgarisms. It is surely far better for a town to be called Los Angeles, Pasadena, or San Francisco, than Southville or Jacksonville. Coronado beach and El Plaza del Rey, the playground of the king, are ideal names for a watering-place.

The island of Catalina lies 24 miles off the coast of California opposite Los Angelos. About 30 miles long, and situated so as to act as a barrier against the Pacific swell and the prevailing winds, it forms, with the opposite coast, a kind of large bay or sheltered piece of water, which is always smooth. It is only very occasionally in the winter that a nor'-wester blows into it. It is for this reason, and this alone, that Catalina is the only place suitable for tuna fishing, though there are other islands which this fish frequents.

The island was bought by an Englishman named Banning for a sheep ranche, and has been turned into a summer resort by his two sons; being owned by Banning Brothers and Co., who claim sovereign rights over the whole island, and have hitherto upheld them in spite of several legal battles with the United States. No boat can land without their permission, and the United States post-office is built below high-water mark. There is wireless communication with the mainland, and a boat arrives every day. There is a very good hotel, and the climate is most equable, neither cold in winter nor hot in summer, being quite free from the sudden changes so prevalent in other parts of California. Early in April I noted the thermometer to be 64° at midday and 63° at midnight.

I found Catalina to be the pleasantest winter resort in California, much quieter than the others, while there is always some fishing, even though the tuna do not arrive till summer. Unfortunately, the tourists and the tuna arrive about the same time, the latter usually appearing in June and the former coming in July and August. Arrangements are made by which the little town of Avalon is turned into a "tent city," in which some ten thousand people are accommodated in tents This naturally makes the island for two months a very different place from what it is for the rest of the year. Several steamers arrive and depart daily loaded with excursionists.

The fisherman who intends to try for tuna will have to put up with inconveniences of this kind, but if he arrives early he can employ himself while he is waiting for the tuna to arrive, by trying for yellow-tail, albicore, bonito, and barracouta. The first three are all species of mackerel. The last named can often be caught in large quantities, but gives little sport. All are got by trolling a small herring.

The yellow-tail is well spoken of by the tuna fishermen as being for its size even stronger than the tuna. It is fished for with a lighter rod and 12-ply line. I shall give a description of tuna tackle later; the tackle used for yellow-tail resembles it in general character, but is much lighter. The fish is a handsome mackerel of a dull silvery colour, tinged with yellow, which becomes more marked towards the tail. I saw several landed of about 25lb., but did not get one myself. The largest on record is 56lb.; from 40lb. to 50lb. is not an uncommon weight.

The albicore is another mackerel, blue above, and silver below, with a curious long pectoral fin on each side, about a foot in length. The fish are found in shoals and can be got in large numbers when the angler can find one of the shoals. I believe it is usual to attract the shoal by throwing small herring astern, and when this is done a fish can be hooked at almost every throw. Those I saw landed were about 25lb.

The bonito is like a large horse mackerel, and is fished for in the same manner as the albicore.

There are many other fish that can be got by fishing deep with a bait, notably the black seabass, which is caught up to 400lb. There is little sport to be got out of it, except what is afforded by hauling in a fish of such immense weight All these fish are good to eat.

In my experience, better sport with all these fish can be obtained at Coronado beach than at Catalina Island, but tuna cannot be caught there, though they are known to frequent the Coronado Islands. These islands are too much exposed for the use of the small tuna launches. There are about 7,000 wild goats on the island, and leave can be got from the Bannings to shoot them, but it is not a very high form of big game shooting. They are the descendants of some tame goats which were turned out by the Spaniards for the benefit of shipwrecked sailors, though it is not known exactly how the sailors were going to catch them. However, some amusement might be got in this way till the tuna arrive. There is also a nine-hole golf course.

The launches used for this fishing are very light,

built for two or three men, and fitted with gasoline engines. The best are pointed at bow and stern, so as to go equally well in either direction. There are a few private ones, and some of the public ones are retained by fishermen so as to be ready when the tuna may appear. It might be well for any fisherman to see that a launch is available if the fish should suddenly arrive. Though the tarpon and tarpon fishing are fairly well known, very little seems to be known in England about the tuna, and though I cannot speak from personal experience, it would seem that the sport afforded by the tuna is certainly equal to, if it does not far surpass, that given by the tarpon, in the size, strength, and fighting qualities of the fish. All the information here given was collected during a visit to Catalina, during which period the tuna, unfortunately, did not put in an appearance.

Tuna fishing is of only very recent date, for though the fish was caught by bait on strong hand-lines by local fishermen, it was only in 1896 that the first tuna was caught on a rod and line, and since that time the numbers caught have not been very many. But little seems to have appeared in the English sporting papers and magazines about the tuna. And it would appear to me that anyone who reads the accounts given here will be obliged to admit that this fish must afford the greatest and most exciting sport that can be enjoyed by the bait fisherman It is a most formidable antagonist and one whose capture may be looked on with just pride.

Even the number of those who have landed a tuna is very small; and very few Englishmen are members of the Tuna Club. The tuna fishing at Catalina is carried on under the auspices of the Tuna Club, an American institution which has an excellent object, namely, to protect the tuna and to see that as far as possible its capture is effected in a sportsmanlike way. For anyone can, of course, capture a tuna with a wire rope, and haul him in by main force; but to capture a tuna under the rules of the Tuna Club is a different matter

According to these rules, the rod must be not less than six feet nine inches long, and must not weigh more than sixteen ounces, the line must be not more than twenty-four strands cuttyhunk; and the fisherman must land his fish with unbroken rod and tackle, and without any aid, except that of his boatman as gaffer; and the said fish must weigh 100lb. or over. On achieving this feat in the prescribed manner the angler is eligible as a member of the Tuna Club, and his fish is entered in the books.

Englishmen might naturally object to any arbitrary rules as to the way in which they conduct their sport, but the Tuna Club makes no arbitrary claim. Any one may fish how or where he pleases, and need not aspire to membership unless he wishes to. The aim and object of the club is simply to set up a standard, and, by a kind of moral influence, inculcate sportsmanlike methods in the capture of the fish, in circumstances, where, by the nature of the case, no forcible means of protecting the fish are available. With such an object no real sportsman should quarrel.

The tuna is an immense mackerel, and its general build and shape show capacity for great speed and strength. The largest caught in the annals of the Tuna Club is 251lb., but far larger fish have been hooked and lost. Fish over 1000lb. have been captured by other means, while it is probable that the weight may in some cases run up to nearly 2000lb. The tuna is gregarious and visits Catalina from June to September in large shoals, when the flying fish, which seem to be its favourite food, also appear. In the winter it probably goes south along the coast of Mexico. A shoal is sometimes seen quite early in February or March, but as a rule they do not appear till the middle of May at the earliest, and, even when they do appear at this time, they do not stay long.

The rod and tackle are very important. The American tuna rod is an excellent piece of workmanship. It is made in two pieces, the tip and the butt The tip, according to the rules of the Tuna Club, must not be less than 6ft. long, and fits into the butt just above the reel. It is made of split cane, but with no steel centre, and is very strong and stiff, bending a little only to the very strongest pull. The butt is built very stoutly, and there is no regulation as to its length, but it is usually about a foot and a-half long, and in fishing is allowed to rest in a hole under the fisherman's seat, so that the rod is controlled with the left hand alone, leaving the right free. The advantage of such a stiff rod lies in the fact that a very strong strain can be put on the fish. It could easily be tested, and I should imagine that a strain of ten pounds could be maintained, increased to considerably more in the case of a tired fish. With a salmon rod a strain of about three pounds is the utmost that can be maintained. The cost of such a rod is some £3, or $15, and it can be bought in New York, or in Catalina Island, or Los Angeles

The reel is also very important, and also costs 15 dollars, for it must hold 1000 yards of line. The winder is of the winch form with two handles, for tuna fishermen maintain that they must have this form to enable them to reel in with sufficient force, thus getting some command over the line. The cylindrical knob of our salmon reel is universally condemned. To the reel is attached a strong piece of leather which can be pressed down by the thumb on the line so as to act as a brake, and is very simple and efficient.

The line is a peculiarly American production, known as cuttyhunk line, made of flax, immensely strong, very light and cheap. I know of no line so suited to its purpose, or which, as I have said before, forms such excellent backing to a trout or salmon line. The regulations of the Club provide that the line must not be more than 24-ply, which is about equal in thickness to a not very strong salmon trolling line; 9-ply is about the size of a trout line. The 24-ply line practically cannot be broken by the strongest man, and stands a dead strain of considerable amount. It is also remarkably cheap. A tuna line of 1000 yards costs 5 dollars, and since they are often broken, this quality is a very excellent one. The lightness of the line and its thickness are both, too, very good qualities when several hundred yards are out, and cutting the water at great speed. The line is prepared and kept in good preservation by being rubbed with common yellow beeswax, and by being dried after use.

The tuna rods, reels, and lines, which I saw at Catalina, seemed exceedingly well adapted for their purpose, and were most efficient without being expensive. It was earnestly impressed on me to be sure to obtain the best tackle, and to have a spare rod and reel and several lines in the boat. Great care should be taken of the tackle, and also to see that everything is in good order, as the fish is a most formidable antagonist, and the slightest hitch or weakness will end in an immediate disaster.

To the end of the line is attached a large hook with a herring as bait. Formerly the flying fish was considered to be the only bait which the tuna would take, and they were not always easy to get, but it has lately been found that the herring is as good.

At first the fishing was carried on from a launch trailing a row-boat behind, which the fisherman entered as soon as a tuna was hooked. In this way the fish was more easily followed, but the boat being often unable to move quickly enough, was at the mercy of the tuna, and was practically towed in all directions. Nowadays, a vast improvement has taken place by the introduction of small, smart-looking gasoline launches, the best being pointed fore and aft, moving quickly in either direction, so that the fish is followed rapidly, or run away from when it suddenly turns and rushes towards the boat. The boatmen are smart fellows, and are mostly registered on the books of the Tuna Club. £2 a day is the charge for a day's fishing, including launch and tackle.

The tuna may arrive at the beginning of June in large shoals, pursuing the flying fish, though the date of their arrival is uncertain; but about this time, or even earlier, the tuna fishermen appear at Avalon and await the appearance of the fish. One of the attractions of this sport is the fact that it is done on sight, so to speak; there is no dreary trolling aimlessly about, half asleep under a hot sun. No one goes tuna fishing unless the fish are seen, because it is absolutely useless; failing a sight of them a small gathering of men collects in Avalon who lounge about the hotel and beach. The true tuna man does not as a rule care much for any lesser sport, but awaits the coming of the fish he is after.

A watchman is kept on the cliffs by the Tuna

Club, who signals their arrival. Owing probably to their habit of pursuing the flying fish, the tuna make themselves visible at a considerable distance by their constant leaps in the air. It is owing to this fact that they are locally known as the "leaping tuna." The shoals are often very large, probably numbering several thousand fish. The signal of their arrival often causes a scene of considerable excitement in Avalon; the cry of "tuna" is taken up by the boatmen from the watchman on the cliffs, and there is a wild rush in small boats for the launches at anchor in the bay. Sometimes before tackle is in readiness and launches got under way, the tuna shoal sweeps right into the little bay of Avalon, chasing the flying fish in every direction. It can easily be imagined that such a sight is calculated to fire the blood of the most phlegmatic of fishermen, and, the Western American being by no means a stolid individual, the effect must be somewhat startling.

As soon as possible the launches put out and commence trolling across the shoal and wherever the tuna show themselves. It is by no means, however, certain that the fish are in a taking mood, though in such circumstances it is probable that some fish will strike, but it is by no means uncommon to troll thus across and across a shoal of the fish without a single strike being made. On the other hand, sometimes they will take most freely. It must not be supposed that hundreds, or even dozens, of launches thus put off after the tuna; it is more likely that half-a-dozen or ten would be about the number. If the shoals stay near Catalina, there will soon be a few more as the news becomes known on the mainland.

The tuna takes much as a salmon takes a minnow, and goes off with a tremendous rush, which sometimes continues until there is little of the 1000 yards of line left on the reel. It is impossible to touch the reel except at the risk of cutting the fingers. The fisherman sits facing the stern of the launch, with the butt of his rod fixed in a hole under his seat. If little line is left, the fisherman may put on the leather brake hard down, and try to enable the fish to break his line; or else wait until the end comes, and chance a damaged reel or rod. Unless he has a spare rod or reel in the boat, the former course is the best. It is thought that this course of events, which is by no means rare, is caused by the hooking of a very large fish.

If a fish of about 100lb. is hooked, his usual tactics are either a series of lightning rushes, which must be followed by the steersman, who must be as quick to go astern as to go forward, or else the fish goes off at tremendous speed a few feet below the surface. The tuna never jumps like the tarpon when hooked, he either rushes along below the surface or goes deep. There are 2000 fathoms of water round Avalon. His mouth is not hard like the tarpon, and the hook therefore goes well in; he apparently knows that he cannot shake it out by leaping in the air. Sometimes the hook tears out, but most fish are lost by breakage. It is perhaps more by the skill of the steersman and the quickness of the launch than by the merit of the fisherman that the capture is effected. When beaten, the fish is gaffed.

Many tall stories are told in Avalon of adventures with tuna, though many of them probably happened when the fish was pursued in a rowing boat. In the launches now in use the fisherman has a better chance. The small boats were towed by the fish at their will. It is reported that on one occasion a boat was towed over to the mainland during the night, and was off Avalon again in the morning. Mr. F. V. Ryder, the Secretary of the Tuna Club, informed me that he went off with provisions to a launch that had been engaged for seven hours with a tuna, and found the boatman in charge of the rod, owing to the complete exhaustion of the fisherman. He returned again seven hours afterwards, and found the boatman still struggling with the fish, which was nearly beaten. At the boatman's request, he gaffed the fish, which went off with the gaff and was lost, owing to the hook tearing away. The fish was the largest he had ever seen hooked, appearing to be probably 400lb. or 500lb. Mr. Ryder informed me that he had landed six tuna in one day, and also in one day had lost no fewer than five lines, and had broken a rod and a reel. He stated that he believed only ten per cent. of the fish hooked were ever landed, and that he would not back himself to land more than 25 per cent. of fish hooked. At the same time he pointed out that many who come to Avalon are by no means skilled fishermen.

The number of fish landed in a season from June to September is by no means large; the best year produced 125, one year 75, another only 50, and last season (1905) but 12 were landed and not one over 100lb.

There are several other islands off the coast of California which are known to be visited by the tuna, but the waters round them are too much exposed to the Pacific swell for the use of the small launches which are necessary for tuna fishing, and therefore the waters round Catalina are the only place at present known where this sport can be followed.

It is not known where the tuna go in the winter, but it is quite possible they might be found along the coast of Lower California, a province of Mexico which stretches south from the lower boundary of California, separated from the mainland by the Gulf of California. It is an almost uninhabited country and it struck me that the tuna might well be discovered among the numerous islands and sheltered waters which one finds along its coasts in the winter months, especially as the climate is much warmer. The tuna do not stay permanently round Avalon even during the summer; sometimes they may stay for weeks, at others only a few days. This is probably entirely dependant on the movements of the flying fish.

An American who had caught both tarpon and tuna informed me that he considered the latter fish to afford far the best sport. Catalina Island can be reached from New York in about four days, a ticket should be taken to Los Angeles by the Southern Pacific Railway: from which place there is daily communication. I should strongly advise the fisherman to buy his tuna tackle in New York, certainly not in England; English tackle makers are as yet completely ignorant concerning tuna fishing. This advice does not apply to tarpon. I might mention that Mr. Ryder spoke strongly to this effect.

It is quite worth mentioning that the season for tarpon in Florida is much earlier than the tuna season, so that any one wishing to try for tuna might first fish for tarpon in April, May, or June, and cross the continent at the end of the latter month to Catalina Island, which could be reached from New Orleans in four days.

This chapter is not intended as a full or accurate description of tuna fishing, but merely to bring the sport before the notice of English fishermen to whom it may hitherto have been almost unknown. It is quite impossible to write a good account of fishing when one has only seen the fishing grounds and not actually engaged in the sport itself. But it may be that others may be encouraged from what I have said to try their luck, and that these short hints on the tackle and locality will be useful.

There have been some reports that the tuna have ceased to come to Catalina, being driven away by the naphtha launches, owing to their noise and the oil spread over the water by them. The chief foundation for this seems to be the fact that only twelve tuna were landed in 1905 and no big ones in 1906. It is much more probable that the non-appearance of flying fish or herring was the real cause. A bad season or two may occur in any kind of fishing. The water round Catalina is practically part of the Pacific Ocean and could not be fouled by a few small launches. Nor could their presence affect the immense shoals of flying fish and herring. It is well-known locally that the latter fish do not appear until the temperature of the water has risen several degrees above that of winter, and it is much more likely that some climatic reason has affected the yearly migration. The tuna will no doubt appear again as usual at Catalina.

THE YACHTING and BOATING MONTHLY.

A High-Class Illustrated Magazine Published by "The Field" on the 1st of each Month.

A MAGAZINE of WATER SPORTS, and the Largest Illustrated Periodical devoted to any One Sport in the World; containing Special Articles by the most Eminent Writers on the following Subjects:—

DEEP SEA CRUISING.   MARINE MOTORING.
YACHT BUILDING   NAVIGATION.
   AND DESIGNING.   CANOEING.
RACING.   ROWING.   FISHING.

Price 1/-, of all Newsagents, or 15/- per annum at Home and Abroad.

From the Publisher—

HORACE COX,

The "Field" Office, Windsor House, Bream's Buildings, London, E.C.

BOOKS PUBLISHED BY HORACE COX,

Published Annually.   In Post 8vo, price 1s 6d.

THE ANGLER'S DIARY

AND

TOURIST FISHERMAN'S GAZETTEER.

CONTAINS

A Record of the Rivers and Lakes of the World, to which is added a List of Rivers of Great Britain, with their nearest Railway Stations.
Also Forms for Registering the Fish taken during the year, as well as the Time of the Close Season and Angling Licences.

By I. E. B C.,
Editor of "The Gamekeeper's and Game Preserver's Account Book and Diary"

Price 3s 6d. net

Sea Fishing: Practical Letters.

By JOHN BICKERDYKE.

Most useful book for man or boy, containing everything relating to Sea Fishing

---

In Demy 4to, price 10s 6d net

CHATS ON ANGLING.

By Capt. H. HART-DAVIS.

A well Illustrated Work, beautifully printed in large type on good paper

---

In Crown 8vo, price 7s 6d, cloth

The Coasts of Devon and Lundy Island.

By JOHN LLOYD WARDEN PAGE.

Illustrated with 21 Vignettes by Mr Alexander Ansted, taken in many cases from sketches by the Author, with map.

"FIELD" OFFICE, BREAM'S BUILDINGS, LONDON, E C

DAY'S SALMONIDÆ.

In 1 vol, Imperial 8vo, cloth, price £1 1s. With 12 Coloured Plates and many Woodcuts

British and Irish Salmonidæ.

By FRANCIS DAY, C.I.E., F.L.S., and F.Z.S.

This work is an exhaustive treatise on the Salmonidæ of the British Islands, and will be found equally valuable to the Angler, the Fish Culturist, and the Scientific Icthyologist.

A Few Copies to be had, beautifully bound in Whole Calf, Full Gilt, price **35s.**

In Post 8vo., with Illustrations, price 3s 6d.

The Practical Management of Fisheries.

A BOOK FOR PROPRIETORS AND KEEPERS.

By the late FRANCIS FRANCIS,

Author of "Fish Culture," "A Book on Angling," "Reports on Salmon Ladders," &c

---

A POCKET BOOK FOR ANGLERS AND RAMBLERS.

In Crown 12mo, buckram, 2s 6d, paper covers, 1s. 6d

A MIXED BAG.

A Medley of Angling Stories and Sketches.

By "RED SPINNER,"

Author of "Near and Far," "By Stream and Sea," "Travel and Trout," "Waterside Sketches," "Notable Shipwrecks," "The Thames from Oxford to the Pool," &c

---

Illustrated Catalogue of our Books sent post free. Kindly write for one.

THE FIELD,
THE FARM, THE GARDEN.
The Country Gentleman's Newspaper.

Published Every Saturday, Price Sixpence, by Post 6½d.

THIS paper is devoted entirely to the interests of Country Gentlemen, and is the Largest and most Influential Paper in Great Britain. The subjects are treated in the fullest manner by the first writers of the day, and comprise:—

SHOOTING.	GARDEN.	TRAVEL.
CRICKET.	WHIST.	COURSING.
VETERINARY.	POULTRY.	ROWING.
FARM.	PISCICULTURE.	KENNEL.
PASTIMES.	HUNTING.	ATHLETIC SPORTS.
BEE-KEEPING.	YACHTING.	DRIVING.
ACCLIMATISATION.	STABLES.	NATURAL HISTORY.
FISHING.	COUNTRY HOUSE.	LAWN TENNIS.
RACING.	CHESS.	CYCLING AND MOTORING.
WILD SPORTS.	PIGEONS.	&c., &c., &c.

All the Subjects are, where thought advisable, **carefully Illustrated in the best manner possible.**

"THE FIELD" gives an additional interest to Country Gentlemen, Sportsmen, Naturalists, and others, as it is the Established Medium for ADVERTISEMENTS of the following matters:—

Shooting, Fishing, and Hunting Quarters.
Estates and Farms for Sale or to Let.
Poultry and Pigeons.
Gamekeepers, Bailiffs, Gardeners, and other Servants.
Yachts for Sale and to Let.
Horses and Carriages for Sale.

Dogs, Stud Horses, Stud Dogs, Farm Implements, Farm Seeds, Garden Seeds, New Books, Hotels, House-keeping, and Miscellaneous Articles.

Subscription to Foreign Countries: Yearly, £1 19s. 6d.; Six Months, 19s. 9d.; Three Months, 9s. 10d.

PUBLISHED BY HORACE COX, WINDSOR HOUSE, BREAM'S BUILDINGS, LONDON, E.C.